BETTER HALF OR BITTER HALF

THE 10 PRINCIPLES FOR MAKING MARRIAGE WORK AND A COMPLETE GUIDE FOR SAVING YOUR RELATIONSHIP.

DR. AMIT DAS

To

All my bosses, associates, and well-wishers who made a difference in my professional career.

"It seems perfect today

You and your better half

Together life may

A little bit tough.

Keeping your love alive

Without a doubt or fears

What you need to go on

A happy life no droping tears.

Add a sprinkle of faith

You both smile and enjoy

An act of kindness

Blend it with coy.

Always keep your love real

More than I know

You are my strength my light

More than you show.

Your deep love and sweet smile

I can feel touch

We are made for each other

I really love you so much."

-Dr. Amit Das, Life Coach, Mentor, Counsellor.

Contents

Foreword

"A good marriage isn't something you find; it's something you make."- Gary L. Thomas

The secret of a happy marriage remains a secret.

Dear Readers,

Thank you for taking the time to learn more about finding happiness and harmony in your marriage. This book includes tried-and-true methods for finding happiness and harmony in your marriage, even if you think your relationship could be in trouble. Marriage may seem to lose its romance and passion after a certain point and never regain it. After all, marriage passion may be anything you want to make of it. There is always a chance to bring back the romance and passion that have seemed to have faded in a relationship.

Even after you exchange vows, you still need to work on your relationship. Even the most successful relationships occasionally require guidance on how to handle conflicts, build closeness, or spice things up. No matter if you're thinking about getting engaged, recently married, or an empty nester, the books on this list, published by the best author and subject matter expert, give important insights that might be useful for everyone.

The way you comprehend, mend, and build marriages has been completely transformed by "Better Half or Bitter Half: The Ten Principles for Making Marriage Work". These simple yet profound ideas provide couples with fresh ways to work out disagreements, find new areas of agreement, and deepen intimacy. Anyone who wishes to maximise the possibilities of their relationship should read this book.

This book's goal is to dispel your false beliefs about marriage. Some people believe that once they commit to someone via marriage, their relationship will be simpler. You will learn from this book that collaboration leads to good connections. By comprehending your spouse, working out healthy conflict resolution strategies, you will develop excellent communication skills. This book offers a solid framework for a happy marriage.

You'll discover in this book how you and your spouse may decide on your respective responsibilities in the relationship. The author Dr. Amit Das talks about and emphasises personal space in order to sustain a strong and enduring partnership. You can also learn to avoid "crossing borders" or seriously hurting your spouse's feelings when you're married. This may entail continuing to have open lines of communication, remaining intimate, and resisting outside temptations like infidelity. Setting limits early on might help you steer clear of potential issues. It's a good idea to consider these possibilities beforehand.

This book dives straight into what to expect in marriage as well as how your prior experiences—both sexual and nonsexual—can affect your sex life. Reading the book from cover to cover might be helpful for everyone. A marriage that is sexually rewarding for both of you may be achieved by learning how to discuss sex honestly and freely with your husband. They could not feel loved by you and vice versa if you are expressing your love to your spouse in a way that doesn't correspond to their love language. This book will assist you in figuring out your own language, your partner's language, and the best ways to express your love for them. It's a terrific idea to read this book together. The book provides step-by-step directions for each difficulty, as well as encouraging advice to motivate you to continue improving your relationship. This book can reduce stress rather than increase it.

This book helps you develop your conflict-resolution abilities since it is packed with useful tips and techniques. The methods discussed in the book are made to deal with whatever issues you and your partner may have. It enables you to go more deeply into the topics that frequently result in disputes or fights. You may learn how to successfully convey your feelings rather than arguing all the time. In order to resolve the most delicate topics and cope with ordinary marital troubles, you will also look at ways for compromising.

This book focuses on useful behaviours that you can adopt rather than offering a step-by-step manual for improving your relationship.

In order to be a more thoughtful spouse, the author Dr. Amit Das advise you to attend to your partner's needs rather than taking offence at everything they do. The beneficial interpersonal behaviours are explained in detail. Every topic covered in the book is supported by research, proving that certain behaviours are effective. The techniques in this book may be useful for often-fighting couples. The author has produced a straightforward book with actual instances of events and behaviours that frequently result in disputes and conflicts. You can see the positive and negative behaviours that foster or obstruct couples' communication Examining the chapters in this book may enable you and your partner to convey your feelings without arguing by revealing the factors that frequently lead to arguments.

The aim of this book is to increase the likelihood that relationships will last by encouraging couples to express their feelings and wishes. It comprises thorough workouts for couples who are married. Ten chapters of the book are exercises that concentrate on particular relationship issues, such as closeness and beliefs. The activities aid in your understanding of your partner's actual feelings and objectives.

This book's "Better Half or Bitter Half: The Ten Principles for Making Marriage Work" recommendations might increase the closeness between you and your partner. The author offers a step-by-step guideance for reigniting the love in your relationship since you understand that remaining in love may be difficult for many married couples. You might find that reading this book helps you think about what your spouse means to you. This knowledge ought to inspire a stronger, lifetime commitment. You and your partner can talk about private issues like trust, money, conflict, sex, adventure, family, spirituality, and dreams over the multiple date evenings. It is a straightforward manual that makes an effort to liven up the regular marital counselling method a little bit.

Thank you for taking the time to read this book.

So, happy reading and learning to all my readers.

Carpe diem.

Dr. Amit Das

Life Coach, Counsellor, and Mentor.

Preface

"All that matters in a marriage is love, trust, loyalty, commitment, and open communication. However, each spouse must make a personal effort in order for the marriage to succeed."- Dr. Amit Das

Marriage is the alarm clock, and love is one long, lovely dream.

Do you ever feel more like a roommate than a love partner with your spouse? The target audience for this book is those who feel empty or lonely in their marriages. It offers advice on how to discuss your emotions with your partner. The easy-to-use tactics are designed to improve interpersonal relations and foster mutual respect. It also discusses conflict resolution methods, making it a worthwhile read for couples who regularly argue.

If you find it difficult to resolve marital issues without resentment, blame, or irritation, you might need suggestions, so give this book a try. It is designed for couples that respond quickly. The author uses positive behaviour therapy to alter how couples handle their difficulties. This strategy aids in altering behavioural habits that are detrimental to your relationship. You learn how to keep from doing the same things that frequently result in disagreements. This book has a straightforward structure. It has 150 questions that are meant to aid you and your partner in learning more about one another's sentiments. As you answer the questions, you will learn personal information about your partner. Ever experienced disrespect? What does "unconditional love" mean to you? These are the kinds of queries you and your spouse will have for one another. Although the questions have a straightforward notion, they have the power to elicit deeper emotions and address possible issues before they develop.

Marriage is not all fun and games, but it is still worthwhile to enter into and stay in for the rest of your life.It takes daily effort, sincerity, love, trust, respect, a desire to stick together no matter what, and a refusal to give up. It is not something that just occurs. Of course, there are also the required brunch dates and movie evenings. I've put together a selection of some of the most joyful marriage quotes to celebrate and appreciate the spirit of this divine union that marriage is. These quotations reveal the joyful sweetness and bothersome saltiness of a marriage in a way that is sure to touch people.Everyone wishes for a happy marriage because they are beneficial. However, marriage is not the most attractive when people are unhappy. You could find this surprising, or you might anticipate where I'm heading with this. I hope you learn something as you read on, anyway. You may have experienced a lot, both good and horrible. You have gone through both good and bad times as a result of your actions (both good and bad decisions), as well as bad times due to circumstances beyond your control. In fact, you might probably agree with me. Each marriage experiences highs and lows. But why do you remain a unit despite everything? Is it to endure the difficult times in order to relish the good times? Or is there an alternative?

Although marriages are made in heaven, it is our duty to make them successful!

Acknowledgements

At the outset I will thank to my family for supporting me throughout the journey of writing my book and encouraging me to live my dreams- my son has always been instrumental in giving his inspiration to complete the writing of this book. Despite the fact that I am listed as the author of this book, "Better Half or Bitter Half" would not have been published if I had depended entirely on my own talents. To create this book required more than a village—it took a family of dedicated and caring people who were always prepared to lend a hand.

Writing a book while working full-time is no simple task, so I'd want to express my gratitude to my amazing coworkers, who act as mentors and cheerleaders in equal measure. Thank you, too, to the rest of the accumentor team for your patience and unflinching support while I worked on this book!

Thank you to everyone who has listened to me argue for doing everything you can to make your life, including your work life, more progressive. I appreciate everyone's assistance throughout the process. This book would not have been possible without each of you having had an impact on my life in some manner.

Lastly, I would like to thank all the people whom I have been associated, you gave me power. I would like to thank Notion Press for publishing my book. At last thank you all for gifting your time to read out this book.

I'd want to convey my heartfelt appreciation to the almighty god for bestowing his blessings and being so gracious.

ONE

LET YOU BE YOURSELF

PRINCIPLE-I

"Love is like a beautiful flower which I may not touch, but whose fragrance makes the garden a place of delight just the same."
- Helen Keller

A married man's show of joy is understandable. I wonder why a man who has been happily married for 30 years seems content.

Marriage is a journey filled with highs and lows, experiences and priceless memories with the one you love. And if you want to commemorate a significant occasion with your lover, you could be looking for the ideal thoughts to emphasize those memories. Why do people tie the knot? They do this because they are looking for a partner with whom they can share a lifetime of love and pleasure.

Numerous couples enjoy a wonderful life together, are deeply in love, and are wonderful companions for one another. This relationship may also take on the most repulsive forms at the same time. The fact that nobody typically learns about the unpleasant things that go on behind closed doors is one contributing element. You will respond differently if someone walks on your foot in public since everyone is looking. However, nothing is under surveillance in this connection, so anything may happen.

But as you go in your relationship, it's equally critical to continue to build your sense of self, get to know who you are as a person, and find your own interests and dislikes in order to continue strengthening your connection. Long-term love relationships often lead to the mending of passions, dislikes, and differences in sentiments, attitudes, and views. These times of healing are frequently lovely and inspiring for a couple that has worked so hard to succeed.

Hindus view marriage as a sacred connection. Additionally, it is a significant social institution. Marriages are not between two people, but between two families. Both Indian society and the law make an effort to safeguard marriage. The majority of Indian society is patriarchal. Sociologists view marriage as a set of duties between a man and a woman whose union has received societal approval as husband and wife. Adjustment between the two partners is necessary for the system to achieve equilibrium so that one partner's role enactment matches the other partner's role expectations.

Hindu marriage is viewed by indologists as a sanskara with the three goals of dharma (fulfilling religious obligations), rati (sex pleasure), and praja (procreation). Dharmik marriages were those undertaken for the sake of dharma, and adharmik marriages were those committed just for sexual gratification.

The institution of marriage requires patience, self-sacrifice, love, and giving. The seven marriage vows one makes during one's lifetime are referred to as saptapadi by our ancestors. Commitment, cooperation, compassion, care, and less ego are characteristics of a happy marriage. You will feel enslaved if you clutch each other's necks. Walking shoulder to shoulder with each other will act as a sign of unity. You will feel enslaved if you clutch each other's necks. It will act as a support if you two walk side by side, shoulder to shoulder. Therefore, help one another, walk beside one another, and advance. There is a saying that states, "Disputes only start over words." Only via language can individuals have fun. People can only get wealthy through their words.

In order to have a good marriage, you must accept your partner for who they are. Everyone has unique beliefs, ways of thinking, views, and points of view. Thus, it seems to make sense that no two people think the same way. Whether you are from the same or a different ethnic background, almighty brings two strangers together when they decide to join hands and share their future as husband and wife. Therefore, it is accurate to state that marriage is the union of two different sets of views and perspectives. Because of their dissimilar mentalities, a couple frequently handles various life situations differently. These discrepancies lead to conflict in marriages, which leads to unhappy marriages.

- *Is it possible to have a happy marriage despite these differences?*
- *How can you retain marital harmony while resolving issues?*
- *Should you criticise your spouse for their errors? Or is being silent the answer?*

According to Gallup research, roughly half of Americans believe that moral standards in the nation are lacking and that things will only get worse. Their biggest fear is that more individuals, both with and without children, are living together or choosing to remain single without making a legally binding commitment. You may have spent years simply carrying on with your daily routine to support your way of life. Daily chores, errands, caring for others, and household management are all lovely, important, and incredibly noble. However, a woman might sometimes get so overburdened with her daily obligations that she finally starts to make a lot of selfless decisions, which are again frequently essential. However, many women entirely forget how to retain an identity outside of being selfless caretakers for their families as a result of their extreme selflessness.

According to research, couples who pool their finances have better levels of pleasure, harmony, and commitment in their committed relationships or marriage. Researchers also found that relationships between couples with combined bank accounts tended to be stronger, and their interactions were more secure, stable, and happy. Marriage is more than simply two individuals joining forces to start a new life; it also entails sharing duties, including budgeting, expenditure sharing, investment planning, etc. One of the most important success indicators of a successful marriage is sound financial management and investment planning.

The institution of marriage as a whole is witnessing the rise of power couples, in which the husband and wife have substantial financial independence. Financial objectives can sometimes be quite individualised, which is why it's important to combine these goals and plan your financial future together. The secret is synergy. In addition to being a useful strategy for asset management and financial planning, married couples who enhance their financial future may also hold the secret to a happy and tranquil marriage.

Marriages are supposedly created in heaven because God creates such partnerships. Living together contentedly with one another, as opposed to living together for years, is the key to a good marriage. In life, nothing comes easily, and when it does, you tend to underestimate its significance. In order to have a successful marriage, both the husband and the wife must be willing to compromise, stand up for one another when required, and show their love for one another. A plant requires the right amount of sunlight, water, and fertiliser to flourish. Only after receiving everything does the plant begin to develop and produce lovely flowers. Similar to this, a marriage requires appropriate understanding. To make a marriage work, a married couple should spend enough time together and talk about the simple things in their lives. A relationship should constantly be nurtured, and this may be done by expressing "I love you" to one another or by taking a vacation together on a special occasion. The concept of love encompasses both compassion and concern. It takes a lot of courage to support your partner even when he doesn't ask for it and to trust him without even knowing about him.

Don't Lose Your Individuality

I believe that there are two things that you should always keep in mind while you are in a relationship. First, you should never violate the promises you have made to your loved ones, because when you do so, you also betray their confidence. The second thing you should keep in mind is to never put any expectations on your mate. You damage not just yourselves but also other people when expectations are not realised. A relationship is significant when the husband and wife work together to understand one another. Whether you have been married for two years or 30 years, every couple will have some difficult times (be it a love marriage or an arranged marriage). Life will have its ups and downs, but they won't last very long. Always keep in mind that life is just like a narrative. And they lived happily ever after, is the book's final sentence.

According to the NFHS study, just 32% of married women in India are employed. Given that just 32% of married women in India are employed, the notion of married working women is still relatively new. The survey shows that there are still significant gender gaps in India. Additionally, 15% of working women receive no compensation for their efforts. The survey shows that there are still significant gender gaps in India. But the good news is that the proportion of married working women has climbed. The good news is that between 2019 and 2021, according to the latest NHFS-5 study, the percentage of married working women has grown significantly from 31% as per last year's NFHS report (NFHS-4), to 32%. In India, the idea of a woman getting a job after marriage is still somewhat new. Due to their obligations to their families and the home, most women after marriage tend to work less than men.

You may have heard or read claims regarding how having a social media presence negatively affects relationships in the current digital world. Social media has undoubtedly ingrained itself into your daily lives. It could improve your ability to interact with others, but it might also get in the way or create a communication barrier with people around us. Social media may negatively impact your marriage and love life, in addition to your interactions with friends and family. You may come across people nowadays who quarrel with their partners only because they like someone's Facebook profile photo, even if it's normal to disagree or debate with their partner. In this book, you go through some of the ways social media hurts relationships. You may interact with individuals on social networking sites and other social media platforms while showcasing your accomplishments, skills, and private life. With these social media platforms, you may start living an online life where you can be whatever you want. This online existence presents a nice image of you and only shows people what you want them to see. Your personal connections will inevitably suffer when your online life takes precedence over your offline one. You start to contact your family and friends less and spend more time online.

If you tend to do most activities with your partner, set a goal for yourself to try new things on your own. I don't intend to imply that you should immediately start making life-altering choices without first checking in. Self-Importance identity in creating relationship boundaries intimacy, expressing yourself, and setting healthy boundaries with your family, friends, and relationships all require a strong sense of self. It can also protect against experiencing manipulation or resentment in interpersonal interactions. Go ahead and enrol in a class on your own if you want to learn a new skill. Don't wait for your spouse to suggest that you join a gym or adjust your diet; instead, talk to him about it and take action! Whether he chooses to accompany you to the gym or not, The secret to succeeding in this is clear communication. Share with your partner your plans to try new things and your efforts to expand your horizons and grow as a person. But do not hold off on asking him to accompany you.

I know it might be intimidating to enter a strange environment without a familiar face by your side, but having the courage to do so can change your life. Nobody anticipates you to be an expert on your first day, but anybody finds the drive to learn endearing!

You don't lose your individuality if you're in a devoted, long-term relationship. In actuality, the finest relationships are those that support each other's personal development. Let's face it: Your lover first fell in love with you because of who you are! It's exciting, difficult, and perhaps even exhausting to fall in love and build a life together. You could occasionally have a slight sense of identity loss, although this is not unusual. Long-term love relationships often lead to the mending of passions, dislikes, and differences in sentiments, attitudes, and views.

Therefore, whether you're searching for a thought to include in a unique birthday picture book present, phrases to include in your wedding vows, or even just ideas for what to include in an anniversary card, I've got you covered. Due to a sense of youthful independence, the word "marriage" may have developed a particularly negative connotation in several areas of the world today. In certain cultures, young people think marriage is a bad thing. Young people are against it since their bodies are in a specific phase.

Marriage resembles a chain and a bond.

You have a certain method you wish to use. But gradually, as the body begins to deteriorate, you start to wish there was a loyal companion by your side once more.Let's examine the rationale for marriage. You have wants as a person, whether you're a man or a woman. If I had asked you about marriage when you were 10 years old, you would not have understood the question. You could have been a bit hesitant when I asked when you were sixteen because you were debating if I had asked then. You have been considering it since your body began developing in a particular way and hormones began impairing your intelligence. Depending on what transpired in your life between the ages of fourteen and eighteen, your response to my question at the age of eighteen would have been either a resounding "yes" or "no, not now" or "not at all." You have physical, emotional, psychological, social, and economic requirements as a human being. It's possible that people don't want to carefully consider these issues because they fear doing so would ruin their marriage. But these requirements and factors do exist.

There isn't a perfect individual on the globe, so they aren't required for a happy marriage. You require unwavering integrity. Whether or not someone is looking, you should conduct yourself accordingly. Regardless of where you are or who you are with, you should always be who you are. Having developed your manner of being, communicating with others may be enjoyable. Another issue is that there will always be disagreement if you try to get anything out of each other and either you or the other person doesn't get what you want.

Another thing to keep in mind is that you are not getting married for the other person's benefit. You marry because you need a spouse. There won't be any conflict if the other person is willing to give them to you and you live in thankfulness. Don't search for the perfect man or woman. There aren't any. It may be a lovely relationship if you recognise that it is your needs that lead you to seek a companion, locate someone who is relatively suitable for you, and accept, respect, love, include, care for, and take responsibility for each other. Thus, it is advisable to use a few words. Typically, when there is a misunderstanding, individuals would say, "Let's talk it out." This is completely ineffective. Just keep going. Avoid talking about the past or seeking an explanation. When a mistake occurs, it just occurs. Just put yourself in the situation where someone continues requesting an explanation after you make a mistake. It is so difficult to defend or justify oneself. Never put someone else in a bad situation. The friendship ties get looser. It requires talent to make someone aware of their error without making them feel guilty. While occasionally expressing your anger is okay, doing so often will wear you and the people you care about thin. If you're feeling depressed, comfort and satisfy yourself. You are gross if you need to be placated by someone else. You will only experience stress if you seek attention.

When getting married, most couples don't consider their distinct life phases, but this might be a big issue if the partners are different ages. A couple might not stay compatible as they move through different life phases because their personalities alter. An older spouse could not want to start a family while the younger bride is eager to have a child, or he might be close to retiring and want to settle down while she needs to keep busy.

On a lighter note, it was once claimed that a marriage is a 50/50 collaboration, but whoever said that obviously doesn't understand women or fractions!

TWO

YOUR EMOTIONAL INVESTMENT

PRINCIPLE-II

"What greater thing is there for two human souls, than to feel that they are joined for life--to strength each other in all labor, to rest on each other in all sorrow, to minister to each other in silent unspeakable memories at the moment of the last parting?"

- George Eliot

"I apologise" and "You are right" are two of the most crucial phrases for a strong, enduring relationship.

A crucial element that establishes the basis of wholesome interpersonal and intimate relationships is emotional connection. Therefore, it should unquestionably be highly appreciated. Even if you may have everything else you require, a lack of an emotional connection can be a barrier to pleasure and satisfaction in a relationship. Couples that become emotionally estranged from one another have a gap that cannot be filled by lavish presents or admirable deeds. Therefore, it is crucial for both parties to preserve the emotional connection. The good thing is that if you think your connection is fading, you can always strive to strengthen it. I've covered a few methods in this chapter for reestablishing your partner's emotional connection.

As difficult as it may be to accept, emotional connection comes before physical closeness in emotionally charged relationships. In other words, the degree of closeness is influenced by open and honest sentiments rather than just physical appeal. Get ready for the realities of how to maintain a relationship if meeting your soulmate originally looked like a difficult journey. That's because relationships may occasionally be really difficult, messy, and convoluted. The good news is that they typically make the effort worthwhile. To find the route through the relationship that works best for you, you and your partner will need to traverse it together, but that doesn't mean you can't pause and ask for instructions along the way.

Whether you've been together for three months, three years, or thirty years, spending time, effort, and energy on connecting with your spouse is essential at any stage of the relationship. But it's typical to occasionally put emotional and romantic demands on the back burner in the middle of day-to-day struggles and obligations that life provides. But according to experts, it might be beneficial to commit to a connection practise with your spouse in order to rekindle the flame and elevate your chemistry.

People and groups with high emotional intelligence may handle relationships extremely well. However, given the society in which we presently live across the world, a severe lack of people with emotional intelligence is a clear and present risk. If one were to pay attention, the absence of emotional intelligence is strikingly evident in the unprecedented level of relational misery across all domains. Relationships are treated as if they don't matter.

Strong emotional ties make people more perceptive about their companions. You don't need your partner to admit that they had a difficult day. You can tell because you can see it on their faces when they return from work. When they text you quickly and clipped, it's obvious. You can tell when someone's rage is an attempt to cover up hurt and when their defensiveness is from a bad habit they haven't yet broken. Additionally, kids learn how to communicate with you and how to handle themselves when they are having a terrible day.

How couples handle their emotional bank accounts is what makes them happy or sad. Did you know that nothing is the main cause of arguments between couples?

Sharing an emotional language with your partner is like speaking a common unconscious language. It involves remaining aware of their wants and issues and following up when you know they have an important interview coming up or have recently gotten into a fight with their mother. A combination of two personalities strikes a balance between encouraging the other to develop and providing a safe haven for falling. Your partnership is held together by this kind of connection. The X-factor keeps your relationship going strong. It is a foundational element of all forms of love and is both trust and understanding. But not all couples possess it.

Your Emotional Connectivity

- Despite being on opposing ends of the mental spectrum, you can understand one another's viewpoints. Understanding one another's viewpoints shows genuine care and concern for the partner and is a positive characteristic of emotionally linked couples. Additionally, you have a strong emotional connection if you both work equally hard to maintain the relationship. You do not hide your weirdness.
- You could withhold from your spouse if you don't have a deep emotional connection with them for a number of reasons. One is that you might not be able to completely trust them with the knowledge; will you be able to remain emotionally stable? People who have strong emotional bonds with their spouses constantly discuss significant events and divulge information when it matters because they truly want to do so.
- You can't constantly be whisked away on a passionate getaway or have a fancy date night. It doesn't matter, though, if you have

a deep emotional bond with your spouse. It's more about continual friendship than constant chemistry. In reality, emotionally close couples frequently merely want to make dinner together, watch movies, go for a long stroll in the park, or spend time with their children. The little things are just as significant and satisfying as the bigger gestures.

- Both you and your spouse are aware when the other is not upholding their own standards. You will be able to hold each other accountable for improving when you have a strong emotional connection, whether it be by adopting healthier behaviours, letting go of limiting ideas, or refusing to make apologies to a family member when they should have long ago. You can be sure that they have good intentions when they bring up a subject, so pay attention. You know that their criticism is given out of love, and because of this, you can always improve by taking it to heart.
- Your emotional receptivity to one another is demonstrated if your relationship is primarily about sharing the little pleasures of daily life. You are aware that the majority of happiness is experienced as a result of little things and actions. You are in an emotionally mature relationship if you can freely engage in your strangest and most humiliating behaviours in front of your spouse. You can only do this if there is no fear of being judged or embarrassed.
- It's remarkable how many individuals think that talking continuously is necessary for an emotional connection. The capacity to engage in in-depth, meaningful conversations with your partner about topics like feelings, friends, family issues, politics, religion, ambitions, and dreams allows you to feel emotionally connected to them. On the other hand, people who have deep emotional ties may also just relax and take pleasure in each other's company while being at ease. Something so basic may provide comfort and calm.
- You might perhaps remain silent and keep watching TV. That would amount to turning your back on your spouse, which won't

help them feel heard or understood. Consider how you would feel if you conveyed something important to your spouse and they made no response at all. It's likely that you won't feel well. However, you are more likely to feel connected to your spouse if they show signs of listening to you and showing interest in what you have to say.

- Overall, maintaining a friendship based on superficial chats or shared interests is not how to establish an emotional connection. It involves having a sincere, strong sense of connection with, respect for, and care for the other person. As you might expect, a strong emotional bond serves as the basis for a relationship that is truly intimate over the long term.

When couples deposit more than they take out, an emotional deposit is built. In a study of married couples, those who remained married responded to their partner's attempts at emotional connection more than 80% of the time , compared to an average of 20% percent for those who were divorced. How couples handle their emotional deposits is what makes them happy or sad. Partners often doubt one another's motives and feel distant or even lonely when the emotional deposit is negative. However, when a couple's emotional deposits is positive, they are more likely to support one another when they are at odds. They maintain an optimistic outlook on their relationship.

Not all types of contact are created equal in relationships. Some touches are enticing, sensuous, chemistry-filled, and ultimately intended to result in sex. Although there is plenty of non-intimate touching between couples who are emotionally connected, such as handholding, forehead or cheek kisses, back rubs, embraces, and other nice gestures. In a non-sexual approach, this kind of contact is nourishing to the relationship and aids in keeping a connection with your spouse. It's a subtle, powerful way of expressing "I'm here with you," as opposed to merely "I want you." After studying hundreds of relationships, I found that most arguments between couples did not centre on particular issues like money, sex, parenthood, or how to handle challenging in-laws. Instead, and most likely unaware of it, they were arguing over a failure to emotionally connect.

What criteria do you use to determine the size of your emotional deposits?

Simply recognising what your spouse has spoken to you might count as turning toward it. Something along the lines of "Oh, that's dreadful." That breaks my heart, dear. Such a reaction will demonstrate to your spouse that you have paid attention to and value what they have to say, which will strengthen your bond. It's crucial to keep in mind that most actions of turning toward are modest, commonplace expressions of gratitude, comprehension, compassion, and generosity. Even when you just reply, "Oh, great!" in response to your spouse's saying, "Hey, look at the rainbow outside," it is an act of turning toward. In essence, when you respond to your partner's attempts to connect, you are putting positive feelings into your emotional bank account. Additionally, you disengage from your companion when you turn away. Similar to a genuine emotional account, a negative balance is the true risk area, while a zero balance is fraught with problems.

Women utilise dialogue to connect with people, whilst men use it to spread knowledge.

I came to the realisation that couples were actually arguing about how one spouse might not pay enough attention to the other's needs or might not show much interest in things that their other cares about, rather than engaging in fruitful dispute conversations about concrete concerns. After dinner, imagine that you and your partner are watching a TV show together when your spouse learns some unfavourable information about one of their pals. You have a choice between turning toward it or turning away.

Managing Your Emotional Investment

There is no way to quantify couple's emotional deposits. Even though the science underlying what causes couples to drift apart emotionally can be rather sophisticated, you employ a straightforward idea to encourage reconnection between partners:

the emotional deposits . The magic connection ratio of 3:1 is yet another idea you have that is simple to remember. What is three to one? Well, turning toward someone is a pleasant encounter, regardless of how modest or subtle the gesture may be. A turning away action is a bad interaction. These ideas can be simple to comprehend, but to put them into practise successfully takes awareness and intentionality. Here are few scientific strategies to keep your emotional deposits positive going forward. You should remember these things to manage your emotional investment:

- Couples must concentrate on boosting deposits (good interactions) and reducing withdrawals if they want to be happy in their relationship (negative interactions). During a fight, you make 3 favourable contacts for each unfavourable one.
- Couples that are fighting already have a negative mindset, so it seems logical that they would become even more negative during a quarrel. This 3:1 ratio does indicate that, even when arguing, you should still say and do three positive things for every bad one.
- Couples frequently disregard one another's emotional needs out of indifference rather than malice. You must thus pay attention. Couples often ignore each other's emotional needs out of mindlessness, not malice. So, you'll need to pay attention. Recognize your partner's attempts to connect with you and move closer to them. They will feel heard and appreciated as a result. Even though you might not be able to get them all, the more you concentrate on the winning offers, the simpler it will be to spot them and go in their direction.
- Even if you disagree with your spouse and believe that the problem is persistent or insurmountable (because personality differences account for the majority of relationship issues), if you can do those good things during a disagreement conversation, that's three good encounters!
- That seems difficult, don't you think? Try redefining your strategy for handling disagreements by remembering that you

don't always have to be pleasant or too accommodating. But you should face your partner, pay attention, invite him or her to elaborate, affirm his or her viewpoint, and show empathy.

- Consider all the times your lover has embraced you or made emotional overtures to you each day. These can be as basic as texting you while you are at work to express their joy that the important meeting went well or that they spoke with you for five minutes when you were washing the dishes together. The idea is to keep those good deposits in mind and then to thank them. It becomes second nature to be appreciative of and express gratitude to your partner for their support if you can infuse your relationship with a positive outlook on things.
- On the other hand, it affects your emotional deposits considerably more when you're going about your day and are abruptly halted by an unpleasant interaction with your partner. Negative interactions are large withdrawals that happen frequently and can completely wipe out a positive balance, whereas positive interactions are tiny, steady inputs. Also, keep in mind that this isn't the place for extravagant gestures. It is based on a daily schedule of constructive behaviours and interactions. Simply learning that they shouldn't take their regular interactions for granted has a huge impact on many couples' relationships.
- According to one study, the main cause of couples relapsing three years following marital treatment was the intrusion of outside pressures into their relationships. Because of this, the most crucial conversation a couple can have is a stress-relieving conversation. Spend 20 to 30 minutes giving each other your entire attention while avoiding talking about your marriage. The aim of this conversation, keep in mind, is to demonstrate understanding and validation of your partner's thoughts and viewpoint. All emotions are welcome during this dialogue.
- All of these interactions—kissing, holding hands, embracing, and cuddling—provide chances to add money to your emotional investment. The Normal Bar research of almost 70,000 people

in 24 countries discovered that couples who like having sex passionately kiss one another without any provocation, snuggle, and are aware of turning toward. Start simply by taking note of your partner's bids if you don't already have a sizable emotional bank account. Continue turning in their direction as much as you can.

- Do more than just pay attention to your spouse if you want to emotionally connect with her. Express your thanks for everything while highlighting all the beautiful ways she enriches your life. Your wife will feel appreciated if you express it. Additionally, it will prevent her from feeling overlooked.
- Never attempt to address a complaint from your partner. Instead, say that you can appreciate their frustration. If you did anything to anger them, you can even go a little farther and accept blame. And if your spouse is delighted about anything, join in the joy. You feel loved when you are heard and understood. Therefore, the more you do that for one another, the stronger your emotional bond will become.
- Your interactions will help you build your relationship piece by piece until your emotional investment reflects the abundance of affection and respect you have for one another.
- Women enjoy talking, and they appreciate it when their partners take the time to sit down and have a thorough conversation.
- You may assist your spouse emotionally with the aid of this. Your spouse becomes more attracted to you since it communicates that you appreciate his or her viewpoints. Ignoring your spouse or failing to recognise his or her desire for dialogue is the fastest way to erode a relationship. Have you ever witnessed a married couple where there is little verbal communication and the guy merely grunts in response to the better half's questions? These couples look more like roommates than actual partners. Being an active participant in the conversation will satisfy his or her urge to chat and offer all the specifics and sidebars regarding the current topic.

- Make a few little, unanticipated changes to your routine once or twice every month. Surprise your spouse with a short weekend vacation or a date for dinner. The goal is to avoid being bored and to anticipate making new plans with your partner in order to maintain your emotional connection. Spend some time talking to your spouse and discussing brewing matters.
- Don't ignore their want to talk and learn everything there is to know about the subject at hand. Being an active participant in the conversation will satisfy their demand to communicate and share all the information regarding the subject at hand. Your spouse will get more attached to you as a result of this small gesture, which demonstrates to spouse that you appreciate his or her viewpoints.
- The widely held belief in society is that "men are not very adept with emotions." From an early age, men are encouraged to be powerful, rugged, and robust—all of which are false representations of masculinity. Because of this, their emotional maturity is still quite underdeveloped, which frequently bleeds over into their marriages. Many men struggle to emotionally connect with their spouses, which negatively impacts their relationships in the long run.
- Couples feel more connected when they face difficulties and overcome them together. Attend a skating lesson, go dancing, or go on a daring expedition. You will feel more unified since you both took a risk and survived it. Making your spouse laugh is one of the best ways to establish an emotional connection with her.
- To strengthen your relationship with your better half, use inside jokes that you've developed over the years. It strengthens your relationship when you show interest in your wife's interests. When you inquire about her interests and favourite pastimes, she will feel cherished and appreciated.
- Encourage them to pursue something they have been considering for a while as well. You don't merely mean sex when you say physical connection. While strolling, hold her hand or wrap your arm around her while watching TV. Your emotional

connection with her is communicated through all of these non-sexual touches. Both entering and leaving a committed relationship need time and effort.

- How to emotionally connect with your wife and demonstrate to her that one of your greatest pleasures is listening to what she has to say. This may be done simply by sitting down before the evening duties overwhelm everyone and tuning into each other. Do more than just pay attention if you want to emotionally connect with your wife.
- List all the great ways your wife enriches your life. Not only on her birthday, either. Express your appreciation for how effectively she handles the requirements of everyone in the household; how well she looks after herself while having to take care of others; and how considerate she is of your parents.
- Expressing your gratitude for the many thoughtful things your wife does every day can increase your emotional investment and make her feel valued and fortunate to be married to you. It will also make sure you don't neglect your wife since you genuinely see her and everything she does.
- According to research, overcoming a physical hardship as a couple strengthens the bond between them. It seems as though the bonding experience is a result of the adrenaline surge. Take a rock climbing lesson with your partner as a way to strengthen your emotional connection. You'll feel more unified knowing that the two of you took a risk and survived it.
- Your wife enjoys talking to you about her interests and pastimes because it makes her happy. You don't have to become involved with them. In fact, a woman having a piece of her own is advantageous to your relationship. But it strengthens your relationship when you show interest in these pastimes. You will also enjoy watching her face light up as she talks about a new obstacle she overcame in her yoga class or how she managed to upload photos to the website she is creating.
- When you are out and about, hold her hand. As you watch television, wrap your arm around her. While she is doing the

dishes, give her a brief shoulder rub. Your emotional connection with her is communicated through all of these non-sexual touches. Pay attention to this, and you'll see how it works out the next time you and your conversation partner feel totally in sync. That conversation will probably lead you from the table to the bedroom.

- She will want to maintain that sense of community, which is why. As a result, it will give you a way to communicate with your wife. In relationships, emotional intimacy is frequently undervalued. Instead of getting assistance when a couple starts to feel distant, they frequently put it off.
- Creating a shared worldview via travel, projects, interests, and other activities is the key to creating an emotional connection that will last for years. These encounters bring a comfort that creates the greatest foundation. These encounters bring a comfort that creates the greatest foundation. The more history you have, the more likely a strong emotional connection exists.
- Consistency and dependability are key components of emotional connection, so make sure your spouse doesn't disappear for extended periods of time or refuses to communicate with you during the day. You should be able to count on them to contact you. They ought to reply to your contacts right away. You have to speak frequently and see each other frequently. You should establish a routine of when to expect date nights or phone calls; you frequently create default arrangements and alert each other if something deviates from those plans.
- We all have moments of anxiety or stress, and having the support of a loved one, such as a romantic partner, may help us get through these trying times. Finding out how your spouse handles stress will provide you valuable insight into how to effectively help them in such circumstances.
- Who do you inform when you receive important news, such as a promotion or the illness of your grandmother? If you weren't going to notify your significant other first, I'd wonder how strong your emotional connection is. If you and your partner

share a deep emotional bond, they will always receive your first call or text. Without pausing for reflection moments after anything happens, you know everything.

- Relationships are crucial, and being in a toxic one may cost you a lot of time and energy that you might be using far more effectively. Be strong if you need to remove yourself from a toxic relationship; be loyal to who you are and what you believe in; and listen to your heart.
- Exercise is great for the body, but when done with a partner, it can also be sensuous. You and your lover will undoubtedly feel drawn to one another and yearn for sex as you watch each other work up a sweat. Recent studies have found a clear correlation between exercise and greater sexual satisfaction, in addition to the physical and mental advantages of exercise. It raises performance, enjoyment, and sexual arousal.
- Physical and emotional elements both play a role in sexual foreplay. You may engage both by making your spouse feel treasured by nurturing them. You might offer to take care of their hair wash, shave, haircut, or other grooming needs. They'll feel at ease and at ease because of it. But more significantly, it could provide your spouse with the finest possible impression of worth and care. When one feels secure and appreciated in someone's company, sex may be more alluring, and grooming them might assist with that.

On a lighter note, getting married is like removing all except one app from your phone.

THREE

RE-ESTABLISHED TRUST AND RESPECT

PRINCIPLE-III

"If you love a flower, don't pick it up. Because if you pick it up, it dies and it ceases to be what you love. So if you love a flower, let it be. Love is not about possession. It is about appreciation."
- Osho

Treat your spouse in a thoughtful and courteous way.

One of the most crucial components of every relationship is respect. It implies that you and your spouse are on equal footing. Everyone's voice is heard, and none is placed above the others. Couples who respect one another are free to be themselves, with their own interests, ideas, and feelings, without worrying about being rejected or facing retaliation from their spouse. Respect is essential to a successful marriage since it frequently takes precedence over love as the most vital quality. Given that it's hard to have one without the other, this makes sense. But respect may be challenging to measure, particularly as parents' roles and self-respect alter. So, what does respect in a loving relationship truly look like?

No matter how far your relationship develops, a solid friendship will always serve as its cornerstone. You regard one another with human decency. You value their opinions and look forward to their companionship. Even if nothing else remained and there had never been a romantic connection, you would still want to be friends with this person. You could start to believe that you know your mate inside and out as you spend more time together. Nevertheless, this is not always the case (nor should it be).

#Marriage is not about compatibility, companionship, or extracting happiness. It is an opportunity to achieve a union that will open up a greater possibility.- Sadhguru

Respect for genuine connections is innately motivated by the need for emotional fulfillment on both sides of a partnership. The benefits of peaceful coexistence via emotional fulfillment will be denied to the present and following generations of humanity if this fundamental force behind all human growth and progress is ignored.

One of the most crucial things partners can do for one another is validation. A fundamental desire for connection is met when your spouse can hear what you're saying, respect you, and comprehend you. As long as you can respect one another's perspectives, it is acceptable to disagree. Healthy couples recognise that sentiments aren't right or bad or true or untrue. You should convey this crucial lesson to your kids as well. Instead of engaging in a harmful dance because we feel like we don't matter to each other, it helps settle disputes.

Respectful relationships entail questions about one another. They are interested in the other person's needs and feelings. encourages partners to be interested in one another in order to increase respect in their relationships. Marriage should be a two-way street, but this isn't always the case. When it comes to domestic duties, child care, and emotional support, there are times when one spouse must provide somewhat more than the other, or when one or both must step up and take on more (such as in the wake of the loss of a loved one or an illness). The obsession with being correct may be quite damaging to a relationship.

According to a poll, 45% of women in tier 1 and tier 2 cities in India believe that lying, even when it is innocuous, should never be tolerated in a relationship. They think that if you give yourself permission to lie, it will quickly become a habit. One day, all those little tiny falsehoods will spark a major altercation. It is important to realize that lying happens frequently in relationships, even if it is not something to be proud of. Occasionally, the goal justifies the means. 55% of the women polled admitted to telling white lies on occasion to spare their partners unnecessary pain. They said that not every truth had to be spoken aloud. 35% of respondents aged 25 to 30 said they had never lied to a partner out of fear of being discovered and losing trust. Their choice is heavily influenced by fear. They are afraid of being labeled liars forever for a tiny, unimportant falsehood. They worry that eventually their spouse will figure out these falsehoods, shattering their trust forever. Results from the poll indicate that 31% of women said they would never trust their partners if they discovered they were lying, lending support to this notion. 32% of respondents admitted to being caught in a white lie that ended their relationship. Sometimes you don't give a tiny falsehood much thought. However, that tiny untruth can be exactly what ends your long-term union. A white lie caused enormous conflict in their relationship, according to 23% of those over the age of 30, and it hasn't been resolved yet.

Being honest in a relationship is crucial since it is the essential component of feeling safe. Even though you may believe that the truth would be difficult for your partner to hear, they will eventually appreciate it. Small gestures have a big impact, and for couples that respect one another, they come naturally. Your spouse can feel validated and valued by receiving a straightforward love letter, a hug that is a little longer, or a goodbye kiss. One quick and romantic SMS or email every day may make your partner's heart skip a beat without sending their brain spinning with too much technology. Include a personal, touching anecdote in your notes as a crucial strategy to strengthen your relationship. Couples that have this desire experience anxiety and animosity, which over time wears down their connection. When partners respect one another, they may concede when the other is wrong in order to preserve a harmonious equilibrium. Successful couples know how to pick their conflicts because they understand that sometimes being right doesn't matter as much as being close. Although telling the truth might be unsettling, a respectable couple will be unafraid to do so. Because they consider the wider picture, they are able to deal with any anger that may arise from speaking about unflinching realities. Do not be afraid of the truth if you desire respect.

You tell a fib and claim you enjoyed the present she picked out for you if she asks. 44% of males indicated they can take the battle and would rather tell their spouse the truth than lie to them, despite some saying it's alright when a deception results in a romantic moment rather than pointless banter. Is it truly important? According to the poll results, 52% of respondents from Tier 1 cities between the ages of 25 and 30 admit that their relationship includes white lies. It does not specify the connection. Since it has no impact on their partner's life, there is no reason to feel guilty about occasionally lying. 56% of males aged 27 to 35 admitted to frequently telling their partner white lies to avoid pointless arguments. Should you be honest with her when she inquires about whether the outfit makes her appear fat? No, they replied. To help her feel good about herself, you tell her a little white lie.

It's crucial to encourage and interact with your partner. You also can't try to fix all of their issues for them by hovering over them. Respectful couples are confident in each other's abilities and trust one another enough to know when to back off and allow the other to handle a situation on their own. They understand that they cannot solve their spouse's difficulties any better than their partner can. They are aware of when to relinquish control and allow their spouse to handle problems on their own. Successful couples are aware of the need to practise self-care. This demonstrates the significance of improving your relationship with yourself.

Respectful relationships between partners create a positive example for their children. They never argue in front of the kids, criticise the other person in front of the kids, or try to turn the kids against one another. Healthy couples schedule date nights and quality time together so that the children may see that the parents prioritise their relationship. They don't mind making errors. Healthy spouses must teach their kids that it's okay to make mistakes and to apologise when they do. Additionally, since nobody is flawless, it's good to seek help if you need it. Even if accepting responsibility for your actions is important, would you not opt to make a small untruth in order to spare your spouse from suffering unnecessarily?

There are several ideas and viewpoints held by people. Although it is true for them, you do not have to modify theirs. You must develop trust in what you know to be true. You must have confidence in the perspective you have on a circumstance or a person. Start believing what you are thinking. You'll start to realize that your thoughts are more valuable than you initially believed. Similar to how the sun is there during the day, certain facts are self-evident and do not require evidence. One of those things that doesn't require evidence is love. But this constant need for validation from your partners damages your relationships. Bad behaviour is frequently displayed by married couples and can lead to resentment and divorce.

People get married early, experience both happy and bad times, start families, start fighting, and have sex less frequently as they become older. When they are with their partner, they all of a sudden feel lonely. What took place? Generally speaking, if you acknowledge a problem in your marriage and are prepared to take action to change your negative patterns, you can make it work. It takes two people to make a marriage work, though, so if one partner has left the relationship, it may be challenging to mend the relationship. Fixing a marriage can be challenging once one is out of the door.

Lack of communication is the main issue that married couples have. Many couples choose to tolerate issues rather than work to resolve them. They first came to an understanding whereby she would look after the home and children and he would work. Later, when new difficulties arise, they must negotiate a new agreement. The question is whether partners can hear each other out without interrupting or becoming defensive and come to a new understanding.

It's not unusual for one spouse to attempt to influence the other. Trying to modify your spouse would feel like a personal invasion and can make them more defensive, whether it's about how he or she looks or about their core values. One of the key factors influencing the durability and health of a marriage is respect. Respect transcends both secular and religious interpretations of marital intimacy. Respect between spouses is a necessary condition for a happy marriage and a sense of "we-ness."

Two epicentres for respect in marriage—appraisal respect and recognition respect—have been found by clinical research. Respect focuses on the idea that you, as humans, acknowledge the fundamental right of people to have free will and agency over their lives. This is both a juridical and moral conception of free will and the right to make your own decisions. Recognition Respect is based on the fundamental principles of freedom of speech, opinion, and action. In emotionally abusive relationships, when one partner's freedom and independence are often put at the discretion of the other, this form of respect is basically absent.

In order to establish and maintain respect in a marriage, there are four essential elements. They are reciprocity, acceptance, accommodation, and mutuality. Mutuality is characterised as the "ground rules" of the partnership. Mutuality controls the power balance like a thermostat. It is how the couples come to a shared understanding of what is appropriate in their marriage. Recognition, respect, and the free will of a mutually entered into understanding are all taken for granted by mutuality. The doable "virtuous circle" of "give and take" is reciprocity. In reciprocity, fairness and balance are sought. Similar to mutuality, reciprocity increases respect by taking into account the distribution of power and influence. The vector of where the idea of respect is heading in any specific connection is completed by the appraisal of respect. Respect is evaluated according to one's capacity for both exerting and receiving influence. The "give and take" of marriage is described. Respect in the eyes of others is a sign of marital connection of a high calibre. The degree of appraisal respect increases with the couple's degree of attachment to one another.

The centre of appraisal and respect is behaviour. The moral component of behaviour is what moves a relationship toward higher levels of appraisal respect. Trustworthiness, openness to influence and listening, loving concern and thinking, patience, and acceptance are all traits that improve appraisal and respect. It is helpful to conceive of appraisal respect as requiring the display of martial values, whereas recognition respect is necessary. The quality of attachment is driven by the positive or negative impact of marital behaviors. Respect is capable of flowing both ways. Respect is reciprocated by being given more respect in return. Disrespect can function in a similar way. Respect dynamics can create negative or positive feedback loops.

How To Treat Your Spouse With Respect?

- Recognize that you married a person who was not ideal.
- Maintain a constructive mindset. Congratulate your partner when they accomplish something correctly or show thoughtfulness.
- Build them up in front of your children, extended family, and social circle.
- Be careful and thoughtful when you speak. Talk to your lover as though you really do love them.
- Do modest things frequently. The tiny things you do may have a big impact on whether someone has a favourable or negative

attitude.

- Observe the four Ts. tempo, topic, tone, and task. How would you phrase that? (Tone). Are you being neutral or are you making your spouse the issue, depending on what you're saying? (Topic). Are you waiting till they come home to attack them, or are you enquiring as to the best moment to do so? (Timing). What exactly are you hoping to have instead of a haven? What result would you prefer? (Task).
- Specify your ground rules. What are the shared ideals that everyone in your family agrees upon
- Can you offer and accept it? Do random, mindless acts of kindness. Don't look for an excuse to be considerate and courteous.
- Set limits to sustain respect in your marriage. Make sure there are no ambiguities that might make either of you feel disrespectful. Make repair attempts.
- Give in order to receive. Keep in mind that being accommodating leads to respect.
- Expect fairness in return by acting fairly.
- Hold regular generative conversations. They will clear up misunderstandings and deepen dialogue about the crucial issues in your marriage.
- Be appreciative of your mate. Make sure everyone knows how awesome they are. Tell your spouse as well. But don't forget to add, "Please do more of what you did; I appreciate it!"
- It takes force to show respect. Every time you materialise it, it will get stronger if you keep working on it.
- The institution of marriage is beautiful, and married people should cherish and love it. However, when two individuals get married, their lives undergo a lot of adjustments.
- Disputes and disputes between the two are inevitable, but they may be resolved via communication.
- The level of respect you show each other is the most crucial area in which you will need to improve if you want your marriage to succeed.

- Respect for one another in a marriage is crucial since it shows support, trust, and the understanding that you both value and adore one another for who you are. Respect for one another is the cornerstone of every good marriage.
- Conflicts between a couple will ultimately result from an unrespectful relationship. If a husband and wife don't respect one another, their closeness will likewise wane.
- It is rude to bring up your husband's faults in front of other people, regardless of whether you are discussing them with your mother, sister, or closest friend. It is far more polite to speak with your husband directly if you have a complaint about him.
- Every success your spouse has, no matter how great or small, in business or in his personal life, should be a cause for celebration. He will be pleased when you share his happiness, and he will know that you genuinely love and respect him.
- Men are more appreciative of physical contact than we give them credit for, and not just in a sexual setting. Even simple acts of affection for your husband would be acceptable. You can sit extremely close to him, hold his hand, give him a few unplanned hugs, or steal a few kisses. He'll feel content, adored, and respected thanks to everything.
- When you put all of your efforts into supporting your spouse when he is down, he will quickly realise how much you value and appreciate him. He will notice your attempts to uplift him and recognise your sincere concern for him.
- Most men don't typically like talking about their days as a means to relax, as most women do. Actually, men like to have some alone time to concentrate on calming or physical activities. Welcome him home, kiss him, and give him some space for a while rather than chatting to him or making him talk.
- The last thing you would want to do with your husband is to nag or argue. If you want your spouse to do something, make sure you tell him clearly and then wait for him to take action.
- Avoid saying it again because he could become offended. If you speak to him respectfully, he will feel honoured.

- Treat him with the respect you know he is capable of receiving. Because of how you perceive him, he will become aware of it and make an effort to improve himself.
- Never challenge your husband's reasoning in front of others. This shows a severe lack of respect.
- Don't point out where you know it better or where you disagree with him in front of others, since he can get the impression that you don't trust his expertise.
- You might agree with everything your neighbor's husband did, but you should never compare your husband to other men or husbands. This is one of the most disrespectful things you can do since it will just demonstrate to him that you are unhappy with him.
- How can you appreciate your husband when you feel so worn out from maintaining a household and being very fatigued by the end of the day?
- Don't let this be a justification for not being accessible to your husband. He needs you, whether it's simply to listen to him talk about his day and hear about yours, or even if it's just in bed.
- Men are often tempted these days, so be careful to remind your wife that she is lovely and avoid making her feel inadequate by comparing her to other women.
- Support your wife in whatever way she sees as important, no matter how big or small.She'll feel appreciated by you if you do this.
- A woman may never ask you for anything since her family is always her top priority, whether or not she works. Regardless of whether she is making money or not, you should strive to accommodate her minor requests. Surprise her even if she makes no requests.
- Even a small favour, like emptying the trash can once in a while, may go a long way toward showing your wife how much you value and adore her.
- The majority of women enjoy talking, so if your wife is one of them, you should at the very least listen to her and give her your

whole attention. She will recognise that you do care for her if you pay attention to the tiniest elements of her monologues.

- You do have a woman that genuinely loves you despite your career, interests, and pals. Never forget to set aside some time each day for your wife.
- If your wife begins to question herself or feel incapable of anything, or even if she already believes she is capable of something but you still have your reservations, you must demonstrate your belief in her.
- Talking things out with your wife is the best course of action if you disagree with something she does. Avoid being patronised. She will feel awful if you criticise her. So be careful what you say.
- Most men begin to take their spouses for granted once they are married. That is not what you do. Continue to show your wife love and attention and give her the impression that you value and need her.
- Never talk to others about private matters involving your wife. If your wife is treated disrespectfully by someone else, speak up for her so that she knows you value her and will always stand up for her.
- In order to establish a marriage that will survive, it is crucial to treat your spouse with the highest respect and love, even when it might be difficult to put aside your disagreements or make enough time for each other.
- Make sure you and your spouse have a healthy connection because they will be your companion for life.
- Couples that have this desire experience anxiety and animosity, which over time wears down their connection.
- When partners respect one another, they may concede when the other is wrong in order to preserve a harmonious equilibrium.
- Successful couples know how to pick their conflicts because they understand that sometimes being right doesn't matter as much as being close.
- Although telling the truth might be unsettling, a respectable couple will be unafraid to do so. Because they consider the wider

picture, they are able to deal with any anger that may arise from speaking about unflinching realities.

- Do not be afraid of the truth if you desire respect. Being honest in a relationship is crucial since it is the essential component of feeling safe.
- Even though you may believe that the truth would be difficult for your partner to hear, they will eventually appreciate it.
- Small gestures have a big impact, and for couples that respect one another, they come naturally.
- Your spouse can feel validated and valued by receiving a straightforward love letter, a hug that is a little longer, or a goodbye kiss. One quick and romantic SMS or email every day may make your partner's heart skip a beat without sending their brain spinning with too much technology.
- Include a personal, touching anecdote in your notes as a crucial strategy to strengthen your relationship.
- In other words, caring for your spouse is insufficient. You must also take care of yourself. This calls for consistent exercise, a healthy diet, and adequate rest. Even scheduling routine visits with the dentist and doctor is crucial. You may demonstrate to your spouse that you want to be at your best for them by making investments in your own health and well-being.

Respectful relationships between partners create a positive example for their children. They never dispute in front of the kids, criticise the other person in front of the kids, or try to turn the kids against one other. Healthy couples schedule date nights and quality time together so that the children may see that the parents prioritise their relationship. Finally, they don't mind making errors. Healthy spouses should teach their kids that it's acceptable to make mistakes and to apologise when they do. Additionally, since nobody is flawless, it's good to seek for help if you need it.

On a lighter note, When a man and a woman are married, they merge into one. When they try to choose one, trouble begins.

FOUR

KEEPING BIGGER OPEN SPACE

PRINCIPLE-IV

"When you trip over love, it is easy to get up. But when you fall in love, it is impossible to stand again."
- Albert Einstein

A healthy relationship must constantly negotiate the tension between intimacy and distance.

Relationships need a delicate balance between the push and pull that never ends. You occasionally have similar needs and occasionally have distinct ones. When your spouse requests space, you should grant it since it's entirely natural. The secret is to remain calm and address this situation carefully. You should give your spouse some space since he or she needs to work through his or her emotions. Many people struggle to connect with their emotions, and men frequently experience cultural pressures regarding their emotions. It makes sense that you would feel a bit uneasy when your partner says they need some space. Nobody likes to learn that their lover needs some time alone. You could begin to doubt your own actions and what went wrong. It's possible that you'll begin to worry whether this is the beginning of the end. But experts claim that having more room might be beneficial. Giving your partner some space is possible without alienating them.

To prevent emotions of entanglement or resentment, healthy partnerships learn to negotiate this very early in the development of their romance. Some people who ask for space do so because they want to say goodbye to you politely and are leaving. Not everyone is at ease enough to express their wants, even when doing so may improve the relationship. That indicates a person who values sound boundaries. What did I do wrong? That can be your initial thought when your lover requests some space. Unless you're always watching over your spouse, it's usually nothing.

The world has altered somewhat for women in today's society. For social and financial reasons, she is not required to get married. She can choose. She is capable of managing her own financial and social affairs. Not a century ago, this was not the case. There is now a small amount of freedom. At least two justifications for getting married are no longer valid. The other three must be taken into account. Getting married is not bad in any way. However, if you get married without having a need for it, it is a crime since you will make at least one other person and yourself unhappy. The Buddha once responded to a question on whether or not to walk with a friend by saying, "It's better to walk alone than to walk with a fool." I'm not that vicious. I'm trying to convey that if you can find a fellow idiot, you can probably work anything out. However, depending on your needs and not what society dictates or because other people are getting married.

Couples that are emotionally mature recognise that they do not need to attempt to "fix" the other or engage in problem-solving in order to resolve conflicts. Giving the other person a safe space to express themselves and just listening to their difficulties without passing judgement or being patronising is key. It's critical to consider your partner's request positively in order to fulfil their needs while keeping your relationship intact. Asking them why they need space or what this means for your relationship is the last thing you want to do. One guaranteed technique to establish distance is to do that. It's crucial to clarify for your partner what having space entails. Identify the times and places your partner desires more alone time. Do they, for instance, require a weekend getaway to hang out with friends? Do they require more solitude to refuel? Or would they rather continue texting during business hours solely in the case of emergencies? It's really simple to communicate continuously throughout the day using SMS or messaging applications. However, a greater relationship isn't usually the result of regular messaging. Limiting your messages during the workday is thus a really simple method to offer your spouse more space. Try checking in during the day instead of texting. Simply say "Good morning" or "Hope you're having a fantastic day" to your companion. Even if we aren't spending the entire day with our spouse, making time for these small encounters still shows them that we care and are considering them.

It's easy to put everything on hold at the beginning of a relationship in order to spend more time with your new spouse. You could find yourself spending less time with friends and family as a result. However, maintaining those relationships is just as important as maintaining your romantic one. Additionally, it's a fantastic way to offer your spouse some privacy. The greatest way to give your spouse space is to put yourself through a genuine struggle that pushes you outside of your comfort zone. Your partner's desire for space might make you feel extremely uneasy if you have any unresolved attachment issues from your upbringing.

Although being open and honest with your spouse might be intimidating, doing so is essential for developing and sustaining closeness. So actually working toward mending with humility may lead partners closer toward re-establishing intimacy and connection. This issue is crucial since so many couples avoid contentious topics, which leads to animosity building. When a spouse can admit they've injured someone and makes an honest effort to put things right without becoming defensive, it feels secure and validated.

The question encourages introspection and sensitivity, both of which are necessary for the health of your relationship. Additionally, by taking the time to understand your partner's difficulties, you will be better able to assist and accentuate them. Because of a straightforward miscommunication about how to make one another feel loved, relationships often end in divorce. Since everyone experiences love differently, it's crucial to try to comprehend why and how your spouse loves to be loved in order to modify your communication.

Spending quality time with yourself is just as vital as spending quality time with your lover. Take into account how you might practise self-care on your own in a way that is rewarding and restorative for you. You might wish to schedule some time in the mornings for solitary walks and mindfulness exercises. Or perhaps you'd prefer to spend some nights alone reading or journaling rather than always watching TV with your companion. Setting aside time for self-care demonstrates that you value your health and put it first so that you can be a better partner in your relationship. It is not selfless; rather, it is essential.

Setting limits with your spouse is one of the components of a good relationship.There are many various limits you may establish, but one that is crucial is determining when you two might need some distance from one another. Set clear limits with your spouse for when you want to have yourself to yourself so that you may concentrate on crucial tasks like work or self-care.

Due to the epidemic and living together, you may not be able to physically separate yourself from your spouse, but there are still some modest methods to do so. If you need to concentrate on yourself or your work, you could choose to put on headphones. Maybe you take a few solo road trips to get out of the house or run errands. It's also okay if you both choose to spend your time doing something else, such as cooking or watching TV while your partner is engaged in another activity. Even if we may not currently be able to visit our friends or other family members in person, it is still crucial to keep those connections strong.

Make an effort to connect with your friends, and keep those interactions apart from your romantic ones. We may need various individuals in our lives to talk to about different things and establish different ties with, so it's crucial to diversify our support system.

How much room should we provide each other in our relationships? It's not always simple to respond to this query. You might not always be able to identify the ideal balance. Space has become even more scarce in relationships as a result of the coronavirus epidemic. Even if more time is being spent at home by couples this year, it's still crucial to keep healthy boundaries and give each other space. In this chapter, I'll offer advice on how to use your imagination and give each other the space we all need while we're confined to the same area.

Every healthy relationship occasionally requires some distance. You may still be yourselves by giving yourselves space that is independent from your relationship. You can be more aware of your emotions when you have a physical space or uninterrupted time to yourselves. Sometimes you need some distance from your relationships in order to recognise your needs and the best ways to care for yourselves. By allowing yourselves time to reflect and work through your feelings, you lessen your tendency to snap at your partners or use other bad communication techniques. Overall, having space offers you all the chance to take care of your unique requirements, emotional clarity, and a feeling of individuality.

You must be transparent with your spouse in order to create space in your relationship. Talk to them about the occasions when, how, and why you might require personal time. Your spouse will be able to accommodate you if you are open and honest about your requirements. They may use this as a fantastic opportunity to let you know about the space they also require.It's not a sign that your relationship is "broken" or that you don't love spending time with each other when you say you might need some distance from one another. It's beneficial to be able to acknowledge and appreciate the fact that both you and your spouse occasionally want space.

For instance, even though you might think you're trying hard to make your spouse feel loved by showering them with presents, they could value heartfelt words or embraces more. It all boils down to communication in the end. If you don't communicate your emotional demands, resentment may start to develop and eventually erupt. Everyone has qualities they wish people would value them more for. You may encourage your spouse to be open and honest about their needs, wishes, and expectations by taking the time to ask them what they'd want to be recognised for. You may then focus on being grateful in that way.

When a husband and wife are constantly concentrating on one another, arguments arise rapidly. After the honeymoon period, when everything is perfect, flaws start to appear all too quickly. After the junction, lines only start to diverge from one another. Once more, communication and trust between husband and wife suffer when they are not focused on one another and when their own ambitions diverge. Furthermore, there isn't much satisfaction or value achieved when the primary objectives are to gratify personal cravings. The combination of two souls, two families, and occasionally even two different cultures is a magnificent one. A marriage is the coming together of two distinct worlds with various histories, sets of values, and lifestyles to form an entirely new world for themselves.

Be organic and straightforward. Relationships naturally grow over time. You start to sound a little fake when you try to establish a relationship. When that happens, your conduct changes from natural to artificial. Don't you see it when someone is attempting to impress you? What do you do if someone tries to impress you? Check out what you enjoy; chances are, others will enjoy it too. You want someone to be really forthright, genuine, unpretentious, and honest with you, right? That is precisely what others expect from you as well. Don't make an effort to impress. Then everything turns negative. The best course of action is to be genuine, forgiving, and in the moment. It significantly alters things.

"Every heart sings a song, incomplete, until another heart whispers back. Those who wish to sing always find a song. At the touch of a lover, everyone becomes a poet." - Plato

Schedule date evenings frequently. Going on dates with your partner after being married is one way to keep the romance alive. A partnership benefits from regular date evenings, but if things start to get dull and uninteresting, they should stop. Traditions like dinner and a movie are there for a purpose, but without a mix-up now and again, it may grow dull. You two can both enroll in a class that you both would appreciate, such as painting or cooking. The foundation of anyone's success or failure is their relationships. Relationships and their results are the foundation of our whole existence. Relationships with one's family, friends, coworkers, community, and other people have a significant impact on how one lives. However, at any level of conventional schooling, nothing is taught about managing relationships.

Relationships are becoming more and more transactional, dismissing feelings in favor of straightforward trading for rational and financial gains. When it comes to interpersonal, professional, and societal structures, this trend may be quite detrimental. Someone may be unable to recognise the feelings of others in a relationship if they lack empathy on a personal level. When more intense emotions between two people or groups need to be satisfied or an emotional reaction needs to be effective, one will fail to prioritize effective intervention.

Relationship pressure and maybe even a breakup can result from a failure to act quickly when someone is experiencing emotional discomfort. Lack of empathy has numerous negative effects, including an increase in early divorces, breakups, spousal disputes, sibling rivalry, parental difficulties, teenage conflicts, workplace competition, and territorial warfare. Since these situations set the stage for several similar disputes throughout the social spectrum, the cost of these conflicts is relatively high for both individuals and society as a whole.

It is not acceptable to offer justifications such as "being busy," "no time for tantrums," "complicated behavior," or "pre-occupied" to justify the complete disregard for feelings. Addressing one's own and other people's emotional emotions is essential for maintaining, managing, and protecting relationships. Setting priorities is the key. If one values a connection, there will be a higher importance placed on seeing to it that the other person's emotional needs are met or handled using a combination of reason and emotion. Undervalued or taken for granted, relationships eventually devolve into redundant and dysfunctional ones.

Sometimes, without letting your spouse know, you may just think they should be aware of the issue. But you must be explicit. I frequently thought that my spouse should be aware of the situation without needing to be informed. I now recognize my error. I ought to have said more. Sometimes, you could ignore your emotions because you feel unworthy of having them taken into account and that your partner's emotions are more significant.

You don't have to give up your values to your partner's. You risk losing your sense of purpose in life if you start to base your decisions on what other people tell you is significant in life rather than what you truly feel. The most significant things in your life are those only you are aware of. What will offer you fulfillment in life is adhering to your own morals.

Then don't compromise your convictions for someone else's. Although standing up for your convictions isn't always simple, doing so will make you happier in the long run. If you are not honoring the principles you believe are crucial to your life, you cannot lead a genuine and fulfilling life. You and your partner can have different political or religious beliefs. Maintain your moral compass. Recognize that you will change. that you will develop. You must develop. Life is not static, particularly if you are learning. Both as a partnership and as an individual, you must develop. You could share interests, but you might also have individual interests in hobbies. You must continue to work toward these.

Give yourself permission to occasionally move in circles apart from your companion. Having your own buddies is okay. You ought to have done it. You would have made a better conversation topic. Looking back, You can see how you contributed to the breakdown of my marriage. You always put your spouse first and was utterly committed to him or her. Everyone has a wish list that includes having a happy marriage. But do they really continue to be joyful and happy? Although the answer to this question may seem incredibly ambiguous, it may reveal a lot about your partner's fundamental principles, ethics, and worldview. Additionally, "understanding the distinctive qualities of the memories might help us gain a closer relationship with your companion. These quotations are an accurate portrayal of the joyful sweetness and unpleasant saltiness of a marriage, and you'll either feel your heart prick up or giggle at the irony of them.

On a lighter note, men, after you're married, keep in mind that you should constantly say, "Yes, darling," at the end of every sentence you have with your wife.

FIVE

DIVORCE IS NOT THE ONLY SOLUTION

PRINCIPLE-V

"Lots of people want to ride with you in the limo, but what you want is someone who will take the bus with you when the limo breaks down."
- Oprah Winfrey

One of the main issues in marriage is a lack of communication.

It's possible that when couples cease complimenting one another's efforts or fail to express appreciation for love gestures, their partners will stop performing those once-appreciated activities since both men and women desire positive reinforcement. Couples often feel angry or resentful with one another when this occurs. After marriage, couples frequently experience a change in priorities. It's common for their partner to bear the brunt of the circumstance and for the relationship to suffer from a loss of attention when either spouse diverts their focus from the partnership to other interests, whether they are a profession, children, friends, or other social activities or hobbies.

In India, divorce was never considered until recently. It is awful, but it can happen if anything goes completely wrong between two people and there is no way to rectify it, forcing them to part ways. However, you do not have to arrange it just before the wedding!

If your life feels empty and you have nothing left to give, you cannot contribute to others. Thus, you occasionally need to prioritize yourself. If you find it challenging, start small. Spend little periods of time doing something you like. Think long and hard about what it is that you truly desire. Don't merely disregard your desires. Start the process of incorporating something for yourself. We frequently forget to express our feelings and thoughts in our relationships. But we must communicate this. It could have been really challenging for you to express any dissatisfaction to your better half. Simply put, you felt forced to tolerate aspects of your relationship that you actually didn't enjoy. Though it was often simpler to keep quiet, you occasionally thought that things weren't fair.

Being a spouse seems to alter one's personality as well, especially in the early years of marriage. Marriage alters people's living situations and daily activities. For instance, males tend to become more responsible and introverted than they were when they were single, but women tend to become more emotionally stable. But with time, both became less amicable. The issue is that when you sacrifice yourself for others, you stop being the complete person you should be. There is an omission. You need to keep your personal happiness and wellbeing for the sake of both you and your relationship.

Divorce is a major challenge since it is not a solution; issues still exist after a divorce. The likelihood is high that the divorce will result in even more issues. If you are unhappy in your marriage and believe that getting a divorce would make you happier, you should reconsider. You probably blamed your partner for the issues and demise of your marriage, but life would be a lot simpler if only one person had failed. While blaming others for your marital issues and attempting to alter your partner rather than working on yourself may seem like a practical strategy to reduce stress, doing so will only cause you long-term grief. Moving on only appears to be simple.

"What counts in making a happy marriage is not so much how compatible you are, but how you deal with incompatibility." -Leo Tolstoy

My observation is that divorced people carry over their marital issues into new relationships. The first step in saving your marriage and resolving your marital issues is to establish realistic, acceptable standards and expectations for your marriage. You're more likely to experience disappointment and annoyance if your expectations are unreasonable and unrealistic. This will cause you to act in a way that might result in separation without even realising it. Yes, I'm arguing that your own expectations may contribute to (some) marriage issues and lead to divorce.

The majority of the time, when a couple decides to be married, they are on the same page and have talked about their future goals. The fact that one or both partners alter their thoughts and develop new goals as time goes on, however, is a frequent cause of conflict between marriages. Consider a couple that has decided to wed, purchase a home, and establish a family. After the honeymoon, if one of the partners decides they would rather travel for a year, return to school, or aren't ready for children, the pair may encounter serious problems. While there's no need to bug your spouse or fear that they could alter their mind later, it's crucial to have open lines of communication to avoid unpleasant shocks of this nature.

It is alarming to observe the exponential indifference in today's society toward even family and personal connections. Conflicts at work and in the workplace are on the rise. Religious, regional, and geopolitically-driven conflicts on a global scale are at an all-time high. Everyone can see the results on a global scale, yet there aren't many efforts being made to change the direction. Many individuals believe that this current tendency includes changing partnerships. Divorce is viewed by partners as a way to break the monotony. It's a running joke in our house that it's just like changing your underpants. Living with the same person all the time feels monotonous, and the need for adventure and variety is not satiated. However, marriage is not a video game, and you cannot just hit "Escape" whenever you feel like it. You don't have seven lives with the expectation that if you play the game frequently enough, you will succeed. Unfortunately, since getting a divorce is now so simple, many individuals hurry to get married before rushing to contact their attorneys and asking them to start the divorce process.

Fixing your marriage issues is to make sure that other aspects of your life are interesting and varied, and to stop viewing your partnership as merely another property. Make sure to keep things exciting by planning romantic outings, pleasant surprises, and vacations, and save divorce for last. It is crucial to realise that divorce has a negative side and that finding the fortitude to save what has to be saved is significantly more difficult than getting a divorce. Keep in mind that you once cherished the person you dislike now.

Divorce destroys what takes years to nurture, and regrettably, the only people who gain from it are frequently greedy lawyers who use every available tactic to deprive "the other side" of their assets until there is nothing left of the person's investment, whether it be material, financial, or emotional.

The couple's poor memory was another factor in their divorce. For some reason, somewhere between cleaning, cooking, buying, going to work, and having kids, the same loving couple who swore to support each other "in sickness and in health" lost their excitement. Couples exchange shy smiles with one another when I ask them to describe the most memorable moments in their lives. They forget the happy times because they are so preoccupied with discussing the issues. The good news is that before they "switch off the lights and send the performers home," they search for answers. The bad news is that they are incredibly miserable and experiencing emotional upheaval. If you've seen Kramer vs. Kramer or The Parent Trap you've definitely gotten a taste of what divorce is like. However, a movie can't really capture the emotional turmoil that individuals experience while contemplating divorce, let alone what actually occurs during this traumatic process.

Everything in our contemporary culture is now considered disposable. Our smartphones must be the most recent model. You frequently change jobs; your laptops only survive a year or two; and you move residences more frequently than in the past. Couples who connect emotionally report feeling more confident in their union. If you and your spouse feel emotionally connected, you may relax without worrying that they'll think you're "too much" or damaged. They respond to closeness and vulnerability with more of the same. Oh, and they shared their concerns and baggage with you as well, since you all have some.

Some of the main advantages that emotionally compatible spouses experience include:

- Continue to observe your spouse and make an effort to learn positive traits from them.
- Put your attention on building trust by modest acts, direct communication, and soft awareness of the connection.
- Take responsibility and start a solution rather than leaving unpleasantries and problems on the back burner to show emotional maturity.
- Deal with disputes and complaints in a calm and collected manner.
- Avoid assigning blame or passing judgment.
- Look for opportunities to show empathy and compassion.
- To promote greater understanding, be prepared to reveal your frailties and let down your guard.
- By studying them, you can find out about your partner's aspirations in life.

- Even if it happens frequently, try to be as emotionally accessible to your spouse as necessary.

I questioned the pair. How have you managed to stay together for 50 years? They said that they were born at a period when if anything was broken, they would mend it, not toss it away. It is tragic that while the spouses waste their mental energy accusing one another of causing grief and disharmony in the relationship, they forget that their children suffer in double and treble doses. I have many clients with broken marriages and many friends who have gone through divorces. When I speak with them, they are all aware of how vulnerable and difficult it will be to subsequently repair their children's emotional states, yet they continue to do so.

People who experience a divorce are anxious and worried that their children's needs will be overlooked. If you have children and decide to try to resolve your marital issues and save your marriage, keep in mind that you are saving it for three or more people. Working with so many couples who have marital issues has shown me that it is possible to rekindle the romance and passion in a relationship. Every family is built on pleasant relationships and successful marriages, and families are important.

How to determine if a relationship is poisonous for you?

It's time to make some significant adjustments if any of this rings a bell. No relationship, whether it be personal or professional, is flawless. But in general, a healthy relationship helps you feel safe, content, loved, respected, and able to be who you are. On the other hand, toxic relationships leave you feeling exhausted, empty, and occasionally even distressed. The last thing you need is a poisonous relationship, whether you're operating a business, collaborating with a partner, leading an organisation, or overseeing a team.

Here are some indicators of a poisonous relationship to help you spot it:

- You will be in the wrong in any connection if you sense energy withdrawals rather than deposits.
- It's time to reassess if you always feel cognitively, emotionally, and even physically exhausted rather than joyful and productive.
- Persistent unreliability and mutual dependability is crucial to establishing trust and is the foundation of every successful partnership.
- It is hard to attain any sort of balance if the other party's interest in the relationship is truly just a reflection of him or herself.
- A negative connection makes it very difficult for anything positive to emerge.
- There can be no connection without communication.
- A successful partnership must initially have respect for one another.
- You may stay in a relationship without trust for as long as you like, but it won't move forward.
- Constant resentment is a surefire indicator of an unhealthy connection.
- Being around hatred should never be done since it makes you feel unsafe.
- Relationships that are one-sided will never be successful.
- Criticism in judgemental relationships is meant to degrade rather than to help.
- You're definitely using too much energy managing the relationship if one person is in charge or there is a continual tug-of-war going on.
- Healthy connections make your life better; they don't make it more chaotic.
- You know you're in a bad relationship when you find yourself altering your beliefs to appease someone else.
- You already know all you need to know if you spend your time avoiding one another.
- All relationships experience difficulties, yet healthy couples manage to overcome them.

- Negative relationships have a sneaky way of making you feel as though you don't deserve better.
- A partnership fails a key criteria if it can't provide comfort.
- You cannot afford to be cut off from opportunities for growth and education.
- Cutting shortcuts or settling for inferior products is never worthwhile.
- Continuous criticism never made anyone better; it serves only to inflate the ego of the critic rather than to improve anything.
- It brings out the worst in people. You can not be your best self if you are always doing badly.
- If you are unable to do anything correctly, the relationship may not be suited for you.
- Not all smiles indicate that everything is OK.
- Every falsehood told between couples weakens the bond a little bit.
- You owe it to yourself to get rid of someone who consistently brings you down.
- Sometimes your heart already knows what your intellect needs more time to figure out.
- You may gradually start to tolerate things that were formerly unacceptable if we are in toxic relationships.
- When there is no certainty, moving ahead seems difficult.
- Although partners will never be completely equal, this fact should be a source of strength rather than disruptive envy.
- Any person in a relationship should be able to refuse an offer.
- If you are connected to someone who is still in the past, you cannot move on.
- When it lowers your sense of worth.
- It might be difficult to perceive your value when you're in a relationship with someone who doesn't accept you for who you are.

My observation is that divorced people carry over their marital issues into new relationships. The first step in saving your marriage and resolving your marital issues is to establish realistic, acceptable standards and expectations for your marriage. You're more likely to experience disappointment and annoyance if your expectations are unreasonable and unrealistic. This will cause you to act in a way that might result in separation without even realising it. Yes, I'm arguing that your own expectations may contribute to (some) marriage issues and lead to divorce. The second stage in resolving marital issues is to regularly remind each other of your pledges to one another. Continue to focus on your relationship so that, despite your hard work, cleaning, and dishwashing, the happy memories of your partnership won't vanish. If you don't think back on the positive, you'll give the negative greater room, attention, and emphasis. The good needs to outweigh the negative for a couple to feel that their union is worthwhile.

Reasons for Divorce or Separation

1. Infidelity or unfaithfulness
2. Money or lack of fulfillment
3. Lack of communication
4. Constant Arguing
5. Weight gain and unfitness
6. Unrealistic expectation
7. Lack of Equality
8. Not being preaopred for marriage
9. mental and physical abuse
10. Getting in for the wrong reasons
11. Lack of individuality
12. Becoming lost in the roles
13. Not having a shared vision of success
14. The intimacy disappears
15. Inability to resolve conflicts
16. Being out of touch
17. Differences in sexual libido or desire
18. Blended family
19. Childrens from past marriages

20. Interfering ex- partners
21. Intrusive parents
22. Difference in resolving conflict
23. Difference in communication
24. Privacy problems
25. Unreasonable behaviour
26. Dissertation/ long standing
27. No premarital education
28. Premarital sex
29. premarital affair
30. Religious differences
31. Lack of support from parents
32. Consistent health issue
33. Domestic violence
34. Substance abuse
35. Getting married too young
36. Lack of commitment
37. One party wanted children the other did not
38. Accountability
39. Attention
40. Work commitment
41. Abuse of alcohol and drug
42. Relocation
43. Nothing left in common
44. Significant physical differences
45. Life Stages
46. Prolong stress
47. OCD
48. PSTD
49. Show Off
50. Boredom
51. Jealousy
52. Lack of responsibility from one partner
53. Addiction
54. Excessive use of Socual media

55. Chatting
56. Excessive reliance on social media friends
57. Manipulation or over-involvement
58. Micromanaging
59. Lack of trust
60. One sided lack of responsibility
61. Perceived lack of concern care
62. Personal disappointment
63. Cultural diffrences
64. Language barriers
65. Ideological differences in parenting
66. Lack of support during pregnancy
67. Physical apperances
68. Lack of compatibility
69. Lack of empathy and sympathy
70. Lack of mutual respect
71. Irreconcilable differences
72. Extraordinary situation
73. Unhappiness
74. Lack of patience and kindness
75. Third party intrusion
76. Tolerating boastfulness
77. Prideful and arrogant
78. Rudeness in accepting facts
79. Selfishness
80. Anger
81. Keeping records of wrongs
82. Cant protect each other
83. Lack of hopes
84. Not willing to persevere
85. Bad friends
86. Hardness of hearts
87. In-Laws invasion
88. Rebound reasons
89. Greediness

90. Ignorance
91. Long age factor
92. Long distance marriage
93. Lack of agreement
94. Wickedness
95. Greener elsewhere
96. Quitters
97. Unforgiveness
98. Criticism
99. Independence
100. Illiteracy

Your romance is usually at its heaviest and hottest in the beginning. You may still arouse that gotta-have-you-now passion, though, so don't let it stop you. This can begin before to having sex, such as by visiting one of your former hangouts on date nights or dressing in the same outfit as when you were first becoming close. Later on in the evening, do a bedtime move that used to really turn you both hot. Begin outside of the bedroom. Rekindling the passion you had at the beginning of your relationship by reliving past experiences is a terrific idea. Consider one of your finest sex experiences, and begin the evening the same way you did then. Reenact your favourite hot moments. This foreplay activity will undoubtedly pave the way for a steamy sack session. Only this time, express yourself the way you wanted to since you didn't know each other well enough or were too timid to do so earlier.

Your relationship might suffer from your partner's constant negativity. If you have been continuously feeling the same way about your spouse, you might want to think about working with a close friend, a member of your family, or a qualified therapist who specializes in relationships. These folks might give you suggestions on how to deal with and get past your uninspiring and boring companion. It is quite easy for couples to relapse into old dispute patterns when they are alone together. Therefore, you need to locate a reliable person to help you break the cycle.

The idea of dinner first emerged in the late 1300s. It was regarded as the primary meal of the day back then. That belief, however, was disproved as time went on and people realized how important good health is. It is the bacon that, in a sense, has taken on that moniker. Because the majority of our daily activities are centered on the modern world, our meals now begin heavy and end light. A marriage is doomed if one partner refuses to compromise and dictates the parameters of the union. Differences in a couple's essential values, such as their preferred religion, can be extremely problematic. It's possible that they will disagree strongly on what religion to educate their kids. Other discrepancies include definitions of good and wrong or other ethical dilemmas, as well as how to discipline. There is plenty of opportunity for discussion about what is good and wrong because no two people grow up with the same beliefs, morals, or objectives. A couple may experience significant issues in their marriage if they are unable to adapt to one another's differing ideals.

In a marriage, financial arguments will always arise. While the other spouse may want to spend, one spouse may prefer to conserve. Conflict over finances typically reflects divergent basic principles. The management of funds must be discussed and agreed upon in order to prevent these issues. It's just a matter of time until the ignored spouse starts to feel abandoned and unwanted if one spouse consistently puts his or her demands before the marriage's objectives and interests. Instead of always having your wants addressed, marriage requires mutual sacrifice.

Everyone defines emotional connection differently for themselves. Genuine support plays a crucial role in creating a strong emotional bond Depending on each person's needs, this support may be either physical, emotional, or mental. Simply hearing what the other person is saying is one thing, but really listening is quite a different matter. It creates a secure environment where the partner may express their frustrations and worries without being afraid of being judged or receiving negative feedback. As was previously said, a good emotional connection is one in which both partners give their partner's needs the highest priority without any sense of duty or expectation. They both have a stake in the success of the partnership. Typically, the following traits identify an emotional connection:

- A connection that transcends mere physical appeal.
- It has the capacity to establish a closer connection with the other person.
- It has the capacity to feel safe while developing an emotional connection with another person.
- A sense of fulfilment and general contentment with the other person.

Don't bring up old arguments that have already been settled. It is preferable to put the past behind you.Recognize that developing an emotional connection takes time. Instead, it is a complicated and individualised issue that needs a lot of work and commitment from all parties involved. Nothing induces feelings of boredom more quickly than a rigid routine that never varies. You don't need to innovate every day; instead, once or twice a month, add a few minor, unanticipated changes to your routines. You enjoy a wonderful marriage and a contented family. However, you feel that by understanding how to strengthen your emotional bond with your wife, your relationship with her may be even greater. Give each other room to demonstrate your devotion and understanding. When arguing in a tense situation, fight fairly and avoid going over the line. Put yourself in the other person's shoes to attempt to fully get their viewpoint.

One last thing to touch on before I close: how should you use social media between both of you as a couple?

Social networking platforms like Facebook increase the risk of people misinterpreting a range of messages posted on each other's profiles, in their photos, and in private messages. You often overlook the importance of body language in communication! Problems arise not only when people communicate with one another on social media, but also when couples communicate with one another. Have a discussion with your partner about what being unfaithful in a relationship entails. Regard each other's sentiments in this situation. In 2014, some researchers surveyed couples and their use of technology to determine the advantages and disadvantages of technology in their relationships. The use of different types of technology, especially social media, resulted in couples' relationships being distant and unclear, which was one of the main issues raised. Some couples spoke of their reliance on different sorts of technology as their sole source of communication during the day. Face-to-face contact would begin to be replaced by this, causing them to feel distant from one another. What's a bit unsettling about this is that you can be doing this honestly to maintain contact without recognising that it's deteriorating your sense of intimacy!

As new social media platforms emerge, you participate in role-playing games, etc. This may need to be continuous. Discuss what it means to use social media in a humble manner. Consider this: if you're married, why are you uploading pictures of yourself on the beach with a six-pack or in a seductive outfit? Who are you hoping to attract? Why do you require that type of focus? Use social media to praise and promote your spouse. This is a huge barrier. Several other couples discussed how using technology to communicate with one another led to misunderstandings since it was impossible to see facial expressions and hear voice tone. When communications were not worded correctly, the intended meaning may be misunderstood. Obviously, the best course of action would be to discuss this with your husband when you get the chance. We are aware of the hurt and resentment some of you are experiencing as you watch your spouse socialising online. That exists very much.

The exact opposite of why you got married is what happens when you are entirely disconnected from your spouse due to social media. You want intimacy, a sense of closeness, and the ability to know and be known. However, with social media at your fingertips and notifications constantly beeping on your phones, all of your open times when you'd typically turn to each other to fill in the blanks are suddenly completely replaced by social media. Consider this. Did you reach for your partner or your phone the last time you weren't sure what to do with yourself? The use of social media in improper relationships and adultery may be the most frequently mentioned concern when it comes to relationship issues.

Use the "Like" button with caution. You get concerned when a young woman shares a selfie or a photo in which it is very obvious that she is seeking approval, and a group of married men immediately jump on the post with the "like" and "comments" buttons. This may also lead to marital resentment! A few people have contacted us to tell us how they almost had physical and emotional affairs on Facebook. They are currently attempting to repair their marriage after they seriously freaked themselves out. You're not against social media, but it's time to acknowledge the significant negative effects it has on marriage. Social media is a relatively new concept. You need to prepare ourselves for it and decide what healthy boundaries you want to set up to ensure that we don't get caught up in something that you didn't expect or want to happen since you don't have your parents to warn you about the risks. Just keep in mind that very few people get out of bed intending to have an affair that day. Instead, you tend to slither or drift into it most of the time, and doing so online is even simpler than it is in real life.

Marriage symbolises a tie and a commitment that is typically made in front of close friends and family. If you want to divorce, you will have to cope with the breakdown of your marriage and the unfavourable feelings that go along with it. The relationship and connection with someone who means a lot to you can still exist if you are able to understand how to salvage your marriage. Additionally, maintaining the relationship might strengthen it and considerably increase your satisfaction.

Do you still recall your initial feelings for someone? Remind your partner of the sentiments and sensations you experienced at the time. Why would a relationship end up falling apart if there was mutual love? Remember to maintain your composure, patience, and optimism. If you and your spouse can mend your hearts and minds, you can salvage your marriage and never worry about it again. Your marriage may be saved, and your love can triumph. Take measures to rekindle your connection. If necessary, seek guidance but take action. You have the power to save your marriage, and that power always lies in your hands.

On a lighter note, marriage is similar to dining out. When you see what the other person has ordered instead of what you wanted, you wish you had ordered it.

SIX

SPICING UP YOUR MARRIED LIFE

PRINCIPLE-VI

"Marriage should not be a social prescription but an individual choice based on the needs of each person. Marriage is an organic process of tying two organisms in such a way that, at least there is a segment of them where they cannot make out which is which – and that is good because they experience some sense of union." - Sadhguru

Foreplay is a great way to spice up your married life.

Physical intimacy is referred to as Runanabandha in Indian culture, which refers to the physical memory of the body. Physical contact helps the body create a strong sense of recollection. Based on this memory, it will respond and behave in a variety of ways. There will be confusion in the body and a certain amount of anguish if you imprint too many memories. People who are careless with their lives and bodies are a good example of this. They never experience true delight. Please keep a close eye on this area around you. They are never able to grieve or laugh completely. They develop like this because having a lifetime's worth of conflicting memories in the physical body leaves a lot of effects.

Living together is not the best way to meet your requirements. Everyone is not required or obligated to get married and have kids. If the human species were in danger of extinction, I would counsel everyone to get married. However, the human population is rapidly increasing. You do mankind a huge service by not reproducing.

Finding the ideal relationship is like expecting the unattainable. Because you have to share so many things in this relationship, marriage can be difficult. Neither marriage nor a man and a woman, or a husband and wife, are at issue. You will have the same issues in every circumstance where you are required to share a lot with other people. You often have to share the same stuff in a marriage or cohabitation. As a result, you step on each other's toes every day in one way or another. In other relationships, you can establish distance if someone is going too far. There isn't a choice available to you. The likelihood of friction increases with the amount of overlap.

Traditional definitions of foreplay include the intimate physical and emotional behaviours that two individuals perform before engaging in sexual activity. But as society evolves toward a more broad perspective on sex and sexuality, the idea of foreplay sometimes seems a little out of date and heteronormative. So many factors Sexual activity is made delightful and even conceivable by the physiological and bodily reactions that foreplay sets off.

Yes, foreplay is enjoyable, but it has deeper meanings. By establishing an emotional connection during foreplay, you and your spouse may feel closer both inside and outside of the bedroom. Not currently involved? It's no trouble! Additionally, foreplay decreases inhibitions, which can make sex more sensual for both couples and virtual strangers. Think back on some of your favourite childhood memories.

The beginning of your romance is usually the heaviest and the hottest. You may still arouse that gotta-have-you-now passion, though, so don't let it stop you. This can begin before having sex, such as by visiting one of your former hangouts on date nights or dressing in the same outfit as when you were first becoming close. Later on in the evening, do a bedtime move that used to really turn you both hot. Begin outside of the bedroom. Foreplay is frequently forgotten, whether you're in a committed relationship or just hooking up for the first time. However, foreplay doesn't have to be that formulaic. For your advice on how to foreplay while keeping things exciting, I turned to be a therapists . The next time you feel a little flirtatious, you'll want to have this list close at hand.

Couples might lose interest in sex for a variety of reasons, from emotional troubles to physical ailments. It's common for sexual issues to set off a vicious cycle where it's hard to want sex when you feel emotionally cut off from your spouse and hard to feel emotionally attached without having sexual closeness. Couples must talk about and overcome their emotional difficulties in order to get past sexual disinterest. The pair growing emotionally distant is a frequent issue in many relationships. When this occurs, it's probable that he or she will begin to gaze about. Adultery can result from emotional infidelity, and cheating is harmful to a marriage.

Every relationship has to talk about and determine what constitutes infidelity. Such horrific relationship abuse's shocking conclusion results in a habit of societal normalization. This trend permanently lowers standards and expectations when it comes to handling significant relationships throughout the social spectrum. While there are numerous, I will only focus on the two main causes of significant relationship suffering in global communities. Compassion neglect Being callous is all but normalized. What else could be dangerous if this is the case? Being insensitive to one's own and other people's feelings has major repercussions.

To aid in the development of an intimate relationship that is mutually satisfying, couples must express to one another all of the foreplay expectations they have of one another. For him or her, sexual foreplay heightens the significance of the sex encounter. But it also improves foreplay between partners by fostering a stronger emotional and physical bond. Intimacy, excitement, and trust are all fostered via foreplay with your spouse or partner. The moment has come to change your methods, even if you can't be bothered with foreplay all the time, in order to benefit from the rewards that will more than pay for themselves.

Regular interactions might get monotonous, but spontaneity can help. It may enliven your actions in the bedroom by bringing new vitality to them. One of the fun foreplay ideas is to have sex in every room of your house. If things grow hotter, you may either take your companion to the bedroom or have sex there and then. There are several forms of foreplay, but controlling the situation in the bedroom is crucial. You can use this to surprise your lover and educate them on your sexual desires and preferences. Here are some fun and wonderful foreplay tactics to get your creative and sexual juices flowing and spice up the bedroom. There are countless foreplay ideas for married couples in various situations.

- Sexual fantasies are frequent, and discussing them with your spouse might help you two become more physically intimate. To bravely reveal one of your deepest desires with your lover while looking them directly in the eye may be immensely exhilarating and intimate.
- The finest pre-play begins in the head and heart. You will observe that investing in emotional connection results in a stronger sexual connection. Most women find that they need to sense an emotional bond's strengthening before they can go from zero to bed.
- Your sexual lives include a beautiful element called foreplay that prolongs the entire encounter. Ideas for foreplay can enhance the pleasure and enjoyment of the interaction for both parties. If anything is lacking in your personal experiences, it is the ideal remedy.

- A passionate, mutually satisfying relationship between the two individuals might be utterly destroyed by a lack of foreplay, insufficient foreplay, or unsuitable foreplay. On the other hand, proper foreplay may significantly aid a couple in developing both a strong sexual bond and a strong lifelong relationship.
- One of the most subtle and heartfelt pieces of sex advice for couples is to give each other kisses and caresses. It encourages intimacy and gives your spouse a sense of security and value. And the desire to be loved significantly contributes to sex foreplay.
- Good foreplay can physically elicit strong emotions, heighten bodily sensations, awaken latent erogenous zones, and prepare the bodies for passionate intercourse.
- For married couples, foreplay is a crucial strategy for breaking up the monotony in the bedroom. There are many wonderful foreplay suggestions that will pique your sexual desire and satisfy you both.
- Mutual touching, hugging, kissing, caressing, and fondling do occur during foreplay, but how you do it is crucial to the process. A harsh, hurried touch, a forced kiss, or a tight grip can entirely undermine any romantic chemistry that could have developed. It can be extremely off-putting and produce an abhorrent revulsion rather than stimulate it.
- By ensuring that your sex is captivating, foreplay assists you in regaining control. Couples foreplay can help you find alternatives to letting nature take its course that will offer you the maximum enjoyment from sex with your spouse.
- By adding physiological and physical factors that heighten the intensity and satisfaction of the sexual encounter, it improves the whole sexual experience. Various physical and mental behaviours that are performed during foreplay might result in more satisfying sex between partners.
- You may rekindle your passion by introducing foreplay into your marriage and other sexual relationships. It may give sex new levels of closeness and ferocity that you might not have

before experienced.

- Regardless of your relationship state, there are foreplay suggestions that might be useful. Tips for foreplay might enhance your sex life with a new person or in your long-term relationship. Erotic foreplay may give your good relationship a new lease of life by providing you with sexy things to do. Additionally, new foreplay concepts can support the development of closeness and trust.
- Consider how something would feel and then explore that as foreplay together rather than attempting particular foreplay ideas. Try experimenting with various settings, taking safe risks, or even the way you communicate with one another. Change up the encounters so that they range from sensuous to kinky, hilarious to erotic, and safe to perilous.
- Make sex more impulsive and sensual by starting it somewhere other than the bedroom. One of the fun foreplay suggestions to create a sizzling bubble of sexual anticipation is to try foreplay in every room of the home.
- Creating an experience using the elements of surprise, texture, creating experiences, boosting intimacy via honesty and trust, taking chances together, and planning for new experiences can all be effective for you. These are just a few foreplay ideas. Ideas for sexual roleplaying will stop your sex life from becoming stale.
- A happy, loving young couple cuddle while having fun in the bedroom. When it comes to sex, anticipation is everything. The big moment is something you're continuously preparing for. Couples frequently develop the practise of starting sex in the bedroom. Maintain the tempo with some sexy discussion, sensual touches, and a few wicked glances at each other, even if you have to wait a while before you can get away, so that when you can, things go off without a hitch.
- There is no right or wrong way to engage in foreplay, and getting to sex doesn't need hours of touching, kissing, and snuggling. You could only require a small foreplay period.

- One's libido can frequently suffer from stress, hormonal changes, and interpersonal difficulties. By employing simulations to get beyond certain hurdles that you might be encountering, fun foreplay ideas can help spark your sexual urge. Additionally, it may enhance your already fulfilling sexual life. Foreplay is the "foremost" and one of the most important components of a man and woman's sexual connection.
- Long before a physical encounter, there is emotional foreplay. The way you connect with each other—how you talk to each other, how you handle each other, how you make the other feel—lays the groundwork for the next foreplay, which can become intensely sensual and passionate when you get physically close.
- Lack of or insufficient secretions (lubrication) can make penetration uncomfortable and even painful, making it difficult to continue enjoying yourself or to have an orgasm and feel satisfied. The "quality" and "length" of foreplay between couples are frequently associated with lubrication. Dryness indicates a lack of arousal, and a lack of excitement is frequently caused by a lack of foreplay that is mutually satisfactory.
- As part of the normal ageing process, the capacity to maintain an erection for a longer period of time decreases with age. To prevent disappointment when a very aroused lady discovers her spouse has lost, it is important to keep this in mind and convey it to one another.
- Sometimes you take the obvious for granted and fail to see it. Despite the fact that breathing is a crucial aspect of who we are, you frequently overlook its potential significance in foreplay and sex. The sound of laboured breathing may make your spouse feel like having sex. Breathe into your partner's ears so they can hear it. Alternately, you may allow them to experience your breath on their skin. It might be helpful to use your breath in a sexy manner while deciding what to do during foreplay.

When new foreplay tactics are included, sex may be more than just physical contact. You may multiply your enjoyment by trying many of the foreplay alternatives mentioned above. Things will become more pleasurable and lively as a result. Sexual pleasure affects how happy a relationship is. Therefore, foreplay suggestions may enhance not just your sexual life but also your relationship. When foreplay is done properly, it may be just as enjoyable as the actual act of having sex. Foreplay is frequently forgotten, whether you're in a committed relationship or just hooking up for the first time. Making a lady smile or, even better, laugh is one way to emotionally connect with her. According to the French, who are known for their seductive methods, "laughter is fantastic foreplay." However, getting your wife to smile is a terrific way to connect emotionally with her as well as a great way to get her attention.

Here are a few tried-and-true suggestions to get you started with your own sexual exploration and spice up your sex life. Build up to it to spice up your sexual life! Create anticipation for your partner and keep them in your thoughts all day.

- Use humour to deepen your relationship with your better half, whether it's through inside jokes based on your years of dating or riffing on current events. Keep in mind that there isn't a set method or model you may use since an emotional connection should come naturally and instinctively.
- You may, nevertheless, use the ideas and advice provided above to trust your instincts and go in the proper direction. You are in the clear as long as the initiative and effort are not pushed. Any relationship must start with an emotional connection. If you feel disconnected from the recipient, no amount of actions or gifts will make up for it. As a result, you need to have an emotional bond with your spouse and care about them deeply. The ability of both parties to support one another, listen to one another, work together, and prioritise one another are some of the characteristics of a fulfilling relationship. Such a relationship may give you a sense of belonging, self-confidence,

and a strong connection.

- Even if you are not too comfortable with the thought of acting, there could be a way to include this amusing foreplay suggestion. Playing pre-purchased video games that incorporate foreplay concepts through roleplay might help you achieve this. Or you might simply dress up. Make the anticipation linger longer by delaying the act and building it up with foreplay sex instead. Do this by flashing your costume at them and letting them know exactly when and how you'll transform into that gorgeous librarian he's getting all worked up about. To spice up your sex life, brainstorm some fantasies and sex ideas you both enjoy on different pieces of paper. Then, you can act out that fantasy with them. This approach to foreplay works well since it improves your understanding of one another's wants.
- Even if there are some things you ordinarily wouldn't do, do them casually and watch your partner's mouth drop. In order to continually come up with new, subtle methods to surprise your lover, do this anywhere you are not meant to. It's a good concept for foreplay that more closely resembles an ongoing game. Seeing your partner's countenance change from one of astonishment to one of desire might be seductive for you. Even while your sensitivities may be sensitive, don't allow your sex to follow suit. You could find that being a bit harsh in the bedroom is enjoyable for both you and your lover.
- Your sex life could be lacking something in that unknown territory. You could have avoided being harsh since it is regarded as impolite and risky. But it might be wise to consider a rough strategy that respects people's limits and is cognizant of them. One of the kinky things to do may be the apparent risk involved. A passionate sex act will undoubtedly begin as a result of the soapy beauty of each other's bodies. What could be more seductive than getting to touch each other while also getting to see one another's bodies?
- The impact of anticipation may be seen in clever teeny-tiny notes that demonstrate your attention and heighten the tension, as

well as in enjoyable games that make you wait for the big payoff. Choose a foreplay style that is both fun and relaxing. It's a good idea to think of it as advantageous for the relationship as a whole as well as for you and your spouse. If you view it as aiding the enjoyment of your spouse or yourself, it may appear self-serving and too much work. Gently caress their face and run your fingers through their hair tickle your partner's insides of the arms, stomach, and thighs. Whatever feels pleasant, softly tickles or rubs against each other. When foreplay is done properly, it may be just as enjoyable as the actual act of having sex.

- The fact that they don't always take place in the bedroom is another distinguishing feature of those intense early connections. You may either have sex immediately or later, take your spouse to the bedroom. You might be shocked at how many sex locations you've been ignoring.
- Uncertain about where to begin? Don't give it too much thought. Sometimes the most effective filthy talk is as straightforward as just saying in your most sexy voice precisely what you want your lover to do to you. Both heat and cold can significantly intensify the feelings you already have. Sucking on an ice cube before performing sex is one of the many (and somewhat overdone) foreplay suggestions for males. Although your spouse may not actually find the concept of a coldness all that appealing, you may still experiment with temperature in other erogenous areas, such as sliding an ice cube down their neck on a hot summer day.
- It's not necessary to restrict foreplay to the bedroom. Foreplay may begin far before the big event, whether it's through passionate texts sent throughout the day or secret kisses given while you're doing errands. For added heat, make fun of one another all day. One of the greatest pieces of foreplay advice you can employ is to change things up if all of your personal experiences are beginning to seem uncannily the same. For instance, if you constantly feel down at night, consider starting a sex session right away. Leave the lights off ordinarily? Instead,

consider lighting candles. Or create a brand new sex playlist. You can alter how you foreplay and have sex, just as you can alter where you do it.

- Sometimes just unwinding is the finest type of foreplay. It might be difficult to truly be present and enjoy being with your spouse when your mind is on a million different things, such as your never-ending to-do list, your boss's mysterious statement this week, and school drop-offs (hence why chilling out is often included on lists of foreplay ideas for women). The best way to unwind is to massage each other sensually.
- Play the game of "growing warmer" while your spouse is lying on their back. Gently stroke various regions of their body with your hands or your tongue. Start with a random area, like the knees or forehead, then work your way up to more erogenous areas. Then they start imitating each other's movements. If they try to take your top off with their hand, you do the same to them. The senses will be stimulated by all the kissing and dry humping, but with a few accessories, you may up the ante. Tickle your companion while they are blindfolded by using objects like feathers, ice cubes, and your tongue to create varying textures and temperatures.
- A person occasionally needs a little more support. The next time you give them a hug or kiss, linger a bit longer and tell them how nice it feels as you slowly move their hands over your body. If their lack of interest in foreplay is due to ignorance, seeing a movie about tantric sex could give them a little push in the right direction. Use items you currently own that could feel pleasant against the skin, or get an internet seduction kit.
- Nothing sets the mood for all the sensual things like candles. Since tea lights are cheap, stock up on them and light them in any place you could find yourself in. Did we mention that candlelight makes skin look good? Everybody has one or two songs that really speak to them in their own unique way. Make a playlist of others, learn what theirs is, and add yours in for good measure.

- For instance, kissing causes the release of oxytocin, dopamine, and serotonin. This chemical concoction raises feelings of love, kinship, and happiness while decreasing cortisol (the stress hormone). Physical foreplay increases sexual arousal, which should not be mistaken with sexual desire, though it can also accomplish that. This actually gets the juices flowing.
- Roleplaying during foreplay gives you the chance to fulfil your wildest desires. When you meet for dinner or drinks, act like you are complete strangers looking for a one-night stand. What about pretending to be a doctor and a wicked nurse? Your choice! Kiss with sincere affection.
- Since having sex at least once a week increases relationship satisfaction, having sex more frequently might make your relationship better. Look for strategies to improve your relationship if it doesn't happen once a week, which is the recommended minimum.
- Your happiness depends on having meaningful connections and receiving physical contact. The best cure for obtaining these essential components for a happy existence is sex. So, how frequently should a couple have sex? The amount varies according to the partnership, but all couples ought to give it top priority in their union. After all, one of the main aspects that distinguishes your marriage from all of your previous relationships is your involvement in sex.
- Excitement and desire might wane with time, especially in long-term partnerships, leaving you worn out and uninspired to begin having sex. You must develop new techniques to excite people about having sex. You are undoubtedly at the appropriate location for that. Read on for a tonne of fantastic stuff. It's critical to keep in mind that human beings need intimacy and connection.
- Sex should take into account both the mental and physical aspects of sexual activity. Simple gestures like caressing yourself suggestively in front of your lover are good foreplay suggestions for both men and women. Make a pattern for them that they can

explore on their own in the future. It may seem harsh to mock your partner without providing them with the enjoyment of a genuine climax, but it is not. It might increase the desire for even greater sexual delight. Make the tension last longer by delaying having sex and building it up through foreplay by using delicate touches and letting them know exactly when and how you'll be.

- Your spouse may be resistant when you bring up foreplay suggestions. They can become comfortable or be reluctant to attempt new things. You may demonstrate to your reluctant partner several ways that sex can be more than simply physical contact. Consider foreplay to be a component of sex rather than something apart from it.
- You might choose a song that is meaningful to your relationship or to your lover. To get them in the mood for what's to come, you may choose a seductive tune. Follow the rhythm's cues! Songs are a fantastic concept for foreplay since they may arouse your emotions. You can tune out any distractions or tension you may be experiencing by listening to music.
- Picture yourself and your partner dancing when you are both close to each other. By putting your bodies close together and raising the anticipation for sexual contact, dancing may enhance erotic foreplay. You may keep the dance lighthearted and amusing if you are first too nervous to make it sensual. Just strengthen your bond as your bodies move in time as one.
- How can you spice up your relationships and marriage with sex? Variety is the key. Try new things to spice up your sexual life. It will keep your chemistry fresh and your sheets blazing if you use different foreplay strategies every time.

Getting married and especially having kids is a minimum 30-year project. If you succeed, at least. If you struggle, it will be a lifetime endeavor. There must be a commitment to establish a stable environment for at least 30 years if you wish to engage in such ventures. Otherwise, you shouldn't start such undertakings, abandon them midway through, and move on. Furthermore, it is unnecessary to discuss marriage and separation in the same sentence as though they are related. Remember, being sexy never hurts. Investigate seductive lingerie selections because they will entice your lover towards you. But more significantly, it may improve your body image and make you feel gorgeous. And one of the finest pieces of foreplay advice might come from this assurance in your appeal. One of the best strategies for sex foreplay is to dress sexily; you can't go wrong with it! It might be difficult to get you or your spouse in the mood for sex after a long day at work. Your spouse may feel less weary and more stimulated at the same time when you move your hands against their body.

On a lighter note, in the enormous store, a man approached a very attractive woman and said, "You know, I lost my wife here. Please speak with me for a few minutes. "Why?" "Because every time I speak to a gorgeous woman, my wife just materialises."

SEVEN

ASSESS YOUR PERSONAL COMMITMENT

PRINCIPLE-VII

"After about 20 years of marriage, I'm finally starting to scratch the surface of what women want. And I think the answer lies somewhere between conversation and chocolate." -Mel Gibson

The Best Method For Relationship Reflection Is Through Questions.

Do you feel ill and concerned because you are spending more and more time by yourself since you think your partner is a pessimist and uninteresting person? Your spouse can feel the same way about you as well, so it's not only you who has this problem. Monotony is the ultimate bore, so it's time to give your relationship a bit more energy. Positive relationship dynamics may be achieved via earnest effort and open communication.

If you are extremely possessive, whether before or after marriage, the other person will leave you. It might not be a good idea to try to possess or control someone. Possessiveness sets off a complete cascade of unfavorable ideas. You frequently like being gratified, placated, and coaxed. So you act unappealing and put on a harsh, unhappy look. Lovers do this frequently. They put a lot of effort into cajoling, which lessens the excitement and enjoyment of the occasion. People tend to flee from people who have a stiff upper lip and demand concessions from others.

There are many ways to reflect, but as was already noted, asking your spouse questions and asking yourself love questions may be a quick and simple way to assess a relationship. These enlightening inquiries about relationships might improve your connections with one another. Or, you may find the issue and solve it by using these questions to ask your spouse. If you think your relationship is deteriorating, some of these relationship questions to ask could perhaps make you feel more at peace. You and your spouse will be able to identify the issues in the relationship and come up with ways to address them via the use of excellent relationship questions.

You should also be posing those difficult relationship queries. Even though dealing with these difficult questions about love might be difficult, they are excellent questions to ask in a relationship since they require commitment from both parties. These relationship-related questions might influence how a relationship develops in the future. A guy values his sense of love, respect, and appreciation at home beyond everything else. This entails making an effort to recall and magnify all of his positive traits. Positive reinforcement will motivate him to keep getting better while also giving him a sense of security and support.

The whole world may believe he has no brains. Always assert that you are the smartest person on earth. Even if you don't utilize your brain, it doesn't imply you don't have one. His ego should always be stroked. Just give him praise and praising from time to time.

Only when both are working toward a common objective for society and the world do relationships maintain their ideals and grow in beauty, love, and faith. Parallel lines continue to travel together indefinitely. Tell him that he has the capacity to perform better, even when he has made a mistake. Even a small compliment can cheer him up. How do you evaluate the current status of your relationship now that you are aware that you need to do a relationship assessment? To aid you in gaining understanding and assessing the condition of your relationship, I have put up a list of 150 questions.

1. What is your most treasured memory?
2. What would your ideal day or life look like if you could construct one?
3. How can couples who are having marital issues resolve them?
4. How can you rekindle your emotional connection with your partner?
5. For what do you hope to be praised?
6. Can you share your biggest sexual phobia with your partner?
7. Can you cry in front of them without feeling judged or open up to them about how anxiety impacts your life?
8. What one aspect of your upbringing would you alter if you could?
9. Is there something you'd want to accomplish or experience together? Would you want to discover or explore anything novel or unusual?
10. What makes you feel better when you are anxious?
11. How frequently do little disagreements escalate into nasty clashes with slurs, insults, and criticism?
12. Do you hold back from telling your partner what you really think and feel?
13. What sexual or emotional desire have you always harboured but never confided in me?
14. What do you find the most lovable?

15. What have you always wanted to do but haven't yet accomplished? What has held you back?
16. Do you frequently find yourself finishing one another's sentences?
17. Do you ever notice how your partner will purchase your favourite dessert exactly when you weren't even aware that you needed one?
18. Do you often find yourself smiling at jokes that nobody else appears to understand?
19. These are only a few instances of non-sexual closeness that add enjoyment and fulfilment to emotional relationships.
20. Can a sex fast increase your partner's sense of intimacy?
21. Is there a point for you to remain together if you can't turn to one another?
22. Are you there due to the other person's influence in your life, or are you stuck because you can't see another way out?
23. Can you work together to make important decisions?
24. Are you a fair fighter?
25. Do the two of you actually understand and accept one another, or do you both want to alter the other?
26. Do you and your spouse respect one another for who we are as individuals?
27. Do you and your spouse encourage one another to be better?
28. Do you both feel comfortable being open and vulnerable in your relationship?
29. What was your initial impression of your spouse, according to you?
30. What did your lover have that you liked or adored?
31. How did the connection begin?
32. How frequently do you fight with your partner?
33. Do you feel content in your relationship or lonely?
34. How frequently do you routinely evaluate the compatibility of your marriage?
35. Is there anything you still adore about your relationship? If so, why?

36. Are you content with the closeness you share?
37. Do you still feel the same way about your spouse as you did when you first started dating?
38. Are you making a difference in each other's lives?
39. Have you begun taking action as a result of one another's influence?
40. How frequently do you share a laugh?
41. How recently have you dreamt of your partner?
42. Do you like socialising with your partner's family and friends?
43. How frequently do you speak with your partner on the phone?
44. How frequently do you consider your spouse?
45. Do you grin when you share a personal story with your partner
46. Do you remember your partner's most passionate moment?
47. Does communication between you two not require words to express how you feel?
48. When has your relationship been at its finest thus far? (Are you grinning as you remember that time?)
49. How do you express your affection for each other?
50. When was the last time you told your lover you loved them?
51. Do you ever make changes for your partner?
52. To what extent do you believe you comprehend your partner?
53. When you disagree, one of you usually concedes, stops talking about it, or ends the conversation. To what extent is it true?
54. How would you grade the management of money in your marriage?
55. Do you feel lonely in your relationship?
56. How satisfied are you with your marriage in terms of the following?
57. How do you feel when people compliment your partner's looks?
58. Do you become envious if your lover hangs out with a buddy who is of the other sex?
59. How seriously do you two take your relationship?
60. Do you frequently bring up disputes, and if so, why?
61. Do you put your relationship before yourself?
62. Have you ever apologised to your partner for hurting him or her?

63. Are you quick to overlook your partner's errors?
64. Do you lose your cool quickly when your partners make little mistakes?
65. Do you have mutual trust?
66. Have you ever stopped your spouse from doing something because you felt envious or furious?
67. How do you feel if your spouse has to be away for a while for work or school?
68. Do you lose your cool quickly when your partners make little mistakes?
69. Do you respect one another's religious beliefs?
70. Is it really important to be fully aware of all of your partner's prior relationships?
71. Do you think you could remain with this person forever, or at least for a very long time?
72. Even though it wasn't your fault, would you apologise to your partner?
73. When was the last time you and your partner had a lengthy conversation?
74. Do you hide anything from your spouse for fear of them discovering it?
75. What should you say to your spouse?
76. Where does your marriage (and spouse) rank on your list of priorities?
77. Do you believe you are liked by your partner's relatives and friends?
78. Do you believe your partner approves of you as you are?
79. Have you witnessed each other's finest and worst sides?
80. Have you ever considered betraying your relationship? Why?
81. Have you ever considered ending your relationship with your partner? If so, why?
82. Are you solely in a relationship because you like the thrill or the sensation of being cherished and cared for?
83. Does this partner help you forget the hurt you experienced in past relationships?

84. Do you anticipate a bright future with your partner?
85. Have you considered wedlocking your partner? (If you two are already married, can you still recall the reason you initially considered getting hitched?)
86. Do you and your partner have the same relationship goals for the future?
87. When you're together, are there more happy than unhappy moments?
88. Do you like to share or sacrifice in a relationship?
89. Would you choose the same relationship if you had a second chance?
90. Are you prepared to give up your happiness in order to have a successful relationship?
91. Where do you draw the line between telling the truth and lying for your partner's sake?
92. Is your significant other your best friend?
93. Do you think of your significant other as your best friend?
94. Is your partnership fair and balanced?
95. Do you lead a separate life from your relationship?
96. Do you two make time for one another?
97. Do you and your partner have open communication?
98. Can you be brutally honest and tell each other the truth, even when it's uncomfortable, or do you have to keep things from each other to prevent conflict?
99. Are you friendly with your partner's family and friends?
100. Can you both set aside your differences and treat them with respect, even though you don't like them?
101. Do your close family and friends believe that your relationship has the capacity to last a lifetime?
102. Are you two able to understand each other's points of view?
103. How often do you evaluate your relationship to see how it's progressing?
104. More importantly, how can you assess a connection to determine whether it has potential?

105. Is there a relationship assessment form you can fill out to see how your relationship is doing?
106. Do you and your spouse have the same fundamental beliefs?
107. What if your political, financial, and religious beliefs conflict?
108. Do you both intend to eventually get married and have children?
109. Can you and your partner recognise and communicate your needs?
110. Do you have a purpose in life that goes beyond yourselves?
111. How forgiving are you of one another?
112. Do you and your partner support one another's hopes and objectives?
113. Do the two of you value one another?
114. Are you two able to converse and express your emotions well?
115. Are you two able to speak effectively and pay attention to one another?
116. Do you and your partner have good sexual chemistry?
117. Does your spouse share your sexual preferences and ideal frequency? What about your on/off switches?
118. Do the two of you appreciate each other?
119. Do both of you feel confident in your connection?
120. Do you work together to resolve the underlying relationship problems?
121. Are you two always preoccupied with your jobs, social commitments, and personal lives? Or do you both manage to intentionally set aside some time for one another?
122. Are both of you team players in your relationship?
123. Are both of you equally devoted to the success of your relationship?
124. Is your partner's concern for you their top priority?
125. Does your spouse appreciate, honour, and accept you for who you are?
126. Do you behave kindly and generously, even when you're angry?
127. Do you respect, honour, like, and accept your spouse for who they are?

128. Do you respect, accept, and enjoy yourself while you are with your partner?
129. How satisfied are you with your marriage in terms of lifestyle?
130. How would you grade your marriage's appreciation and affection?
131. Does your relationship make you feel your best?
132. Is your partner the best person to lean on for emotional support and motivation?
133. Does your spouse have faith in your talents and character?
134. How committed are you to one another?
135. How appreciative are you of one another?
136. Does your spouse support your personal development?
137. Do you feel like a distinct person with respectable values, interests, and opinions?
138. Is your significant other pleased with your successes?
139. Have your partner and you got each other's backs?
140. Can you two talk things through and come to a conclusion together?
141. Do you feel heard, accepted, secure, and at peace?
142. Is your significant other your best friend? Consistently?
143. How much respect do you have for your wife?
144. Do you and your partner affirm each other?
145. How may infidelity-related marriage issues be resolved?
146. How would you sum up your sexual experience?
147. Have you ever wondered why marriage is so difficult?
148. Do you know the different phases of marriage?
149. Why are you constantly looking at our marriage certificate?
150. How "connected" are you on a social, physical, emotional, and spiritual level?

Suggestions

Consider whether the two of you feel heard and supported in the relationship or whether there is a power struggle. While it's crucial to have friends outside of your relationship, research indicates that getting married to your closest friend increases the likelihood that your life will be happier. Building satisfying relationships may prove difficult if you or your spouse lack empathy and fail to appreciate one another's perspectives. Although it would be ideal if you did, it is not absolutely required for you two to get along with each other's friends and family. It's normal if not everyone in your family or circle of friends approves of the person you find attractive. However, if the majority of your friends believe you shouldn't be with your partner, you need to pay attention and learn why. If you and your partner can work through an issue together and delve deeper when one occurs, it can be a sign that your relationship is growing stronger every day.

Trust and security in your relationship should come naturally to you and your spouse. Neither of you should be concerned about your spouse cheating on you or leaving you. A good relationship requires that both people respect one another. Whether you're wondering "how to evaluate a relationship," check to determine if your significant other respects your limits and doesn't overstep them.

According to research, a helpful spouse makes relationships more satisfying. Additionally, it is crucial to have their ongoing support and inspiration while you work to accomplish your objectives. Being appreciative of one another in a relationship is crucial because it demonstrates that no one is taking the other person for granted. In a relationship, effective communication may help you overcome disputes and receive the things you need. Assessing the health of your relationship requires consideration of your partner's sexual compatibility.

Your partners are not mind readers. Because of this, it's critical to examine yourself in the relationship to determine your requirements. Then consider whether you feel free to discuss your desires with your spouse without fear of causing a fight. The majority of your shared values and fundamental ideas should be the same for your relationship to last, even though certain discrepancies may not be a huge concern.

A woman's need to be heard, understood, and appreciated is her first priority. This entails giving her a sympathetic, forgiving, and encouraging ear. You might easily become enmeshed in your emotions since they are so strong. It's crucial for the man to handle the woman's feelings tactfully. You might need to provide them with good care at times. You get the ability to deal with your wife's emotions while still being reasonable and compassionate via meditation. It enables you to create the nice atmosphere that is necessary for a strong connection.

Just as you grow and change as people, relationships too tend to adapt and evolve through time. Before a relationship reaches the "commitment" stage, when partners decide to spend the rest of their lives together, it almost always goes through a number of dating phases. No matter how hard you try, the "honeymoon phase" won't last forever. Because while they are forming a romantic connection, both parties must deal with the ups and downs of life, make difficult decisions, and deal with many pressures. Their relationship and worldview may alter as a result of these events. Therefore, it's critical to evaluate the status and quality of your connection by taking stock of it. Your relationship's condition reveals where you are and whether you need to make improvements to reach a better place. If you're unsure of how to assess your relationship, see if both parties can speak in terms of "we" or "us" rather than "you" or "I."

After you've answered all of these, you might wish to analyse the results to evaluate your relationship. But keep in mind that neither the answers to these questions nor the determination of whether you have discovered "The One" are intended to foretell the course of your relationship. Making relationship evaluations might offer insights if you're unsure how to evaluate the current status of your relationship. It can assist you in determining what must remain the same and what must change in order to maintain a healthy long-term relationship. In a love relationship, independence is essential. You need to test whether each of you can maintain your own interests, follow your passions, and spend time with your friends without making the other person unhappy.

After being in a relationship for some time, you could go through phases where you question if you still have the same enthusiasm for your spouse. Perhaps you are just weary of them as they are, or perhaps you and your spouse are at a different stage of your relationship and you are secretly uncomfortable with it. If so, it might be time to think back on your relationship and pose some important love-related queries. Even if you are currently content with your relationship, reflecting on it and considering relationship-related concerns might help it grow. Nobody of us is perfect. Consider whether you and your spouse often challenge and support one another's personal development.You must ascertain whether you and your spouse are at ease with each other's vulnerability and sharing of sentiments.One of the most crucial things to ask yourself in a relationship is certainly this one.

Any relationship will inevitably experience conflicts, and disagreeing doesn't always indicate that you two are incompatible. But if all of your disagreements are characterised by disrespect, criticism, and nastiness, it may be time to reevaluate your connection. To have a good relationship, both parties must feel free to voice their worries and emotions. Instead of one person controlling the other, You and your spouse should feel emotionally secure around one another in a relationship that will last, and you should know that they'll be there for you when the going gets rough.

Although these self-reflection questions on relationships are intended for you, you shouldn't let that stop you from asking your spouse about them and expressing your thoughts. They might be used in tandem or separately, as the aforementioned categories and those questions imply. The most important thing to keep in mind is that there are no right or incorrect responses. This is just for reflection, since excellent relationship inquiries are designed to point out problems so that you may address them and find solutions.

Long-term, healthy relationships are never simple to maintain, but by attempting to respond to the questions above, you could gain fresh perspectives on your relationship and learn what to do about your love life. As a result, it may result in a greater bond between you and your spouse.

Couples should put their relationship first. The fact that couples are not spending enough time together, in my opinion, is the single largest cause of relationships breaking down nowadays. There is a delay in focusing on the relationship. Everything else appears to be more significant, including employment, families, hobbies, volunteer work, and personal interests. Relationship issues arise when they are neglected. People who put their relationships last tell me that when they do spend time together, they frequently wind up bickering. They dispute over regular problems like unpaid bills, messy homes, rowdy kids, etc.

However, the fact is that disputes about "who is doing what around the house" may be related to a number of other issues. Some of them, such as issues with isolation, loneliness, and resentment, could be connected to the relationship itself. Sometimes the concerns are more socially and culturally based, such as when there are gender disparities, economic challenges, or issues with depression and anxiety. When their emotional needs are not addressed, individuals frequently quarrel over unimportant matters. The empty Coke can in the living room serves as a metaphor for disregard for the relationship. This may sound familiar to you.

The catch-22 is that when you and your spouse are fighting a lot, you don't want to spend time with each other. Unfortunately, avoiding the issue just worsens it: there is more distance, there is more tension, there is less collaboration, there is more conflict, and so on. But time spent with someone else may be a powerful healer. Even though it may seem awkward at first, when two individuals decide to devote time and attention to their relationship, positive outcomes are possible. When people prioritise their connections, they begin to feel valued and significant. They experience love. Spending time with your lover makes it clear to them that you value them. Spending time together allows couples to create new memories, recall old ones, engage in enjoyable activities, laugh at each other's jokes, and rekindle their romance.

Do plan and schedule dates together. Like you would for a work appointment or a doctor's appointment, note these dates in your calendar or appointment book. Do make time for your relationship without the kids. Keeping your marriage together is the best thing you can do for your children. Participate in enjoyable activities with your companion to strengthen your feelings of love for one another. You could even find that you can settle contentious issues in the future with less difficulty as a consequence.Take a stroll around the block. Read a book with a friend. Try dancing (or take dance lessons). Allocate 10 minutes every day for conversation. Don't assume that in order to establish intimacy and connection, you need to spend a lot of time together. Meetings that are quick and frequent also work. Small adjustments to your routine might have a big impact.

Don't assume that spending quality time with each other requires travelling to a tropical island. To express your love for your lover, you do not need to spend a lot of money. Remember that having fun together is a sign that you both understand that your relationship is important and should not be taken for granted. Enjoy the present and the time you have with your partner while you play cheerfully and inventively.

On a lighter note, while there are always shocks in a marriage, most of them include asking one another, "Do you have to do it right now?"

EIGHT

DEALING WITH HOT BUTTONS

PRINCIPLE-VIII

"I'm selfish, impatient and a little insecure. I make mistakes, I am out of control and at times hard to handle. But if you can't handle me at my worst, then you sure as hell don't deserve me at my best."
- Marilyn Monroe

Finding Hidden Expectations In Your Spouse Is The Art Of Relationship.

The majority of disastrous relationships between people, groups, communities, or even nations are caused by behaviour that lacks empathy, by undervaluing the importance of such relationships, or by redundancy. At your heart, you are emotional creatures. Later, on the back of an emotional core, rational and logical thoughts have developed. One is uneducated if they do not realize that emotional satiation is a crucial component of strong emotional wellness. As was already mentioned, emotions are essential to human life.

The first stage of treatment is mostly devoted to assisting couples in reestablishing or developing a more respectful relationship. Once a more respectful setting or atmosphere has been created, therapy may start to concentrate on assisting you and your spouse in identifying challenging topics and figuring out how to directly discuss these difficulties without setting off angry or disrespectful actions. If you want to be able to deal with challenging issues and disagreements in an effective manner, you must first establish a respectful connection. Thus, developing respect for one another is a crucial stage in treatment.

Since you two are now a family, you must look out for one another in all respects, especially financially. In all likelihood, you can both support your existing way of life if you are both financially independent. You must obtain a sufficient life insurance policy if you want your partner to maintain the existing standard of living. Always keep your net banking passwords, debit card PIN, and other important information in a locked folder. In order for your spouse to have access to the password in an emergency, share it with them Both spouses should get life insurance, especially if they are the family's primary earners. If you have made any sizable purchases using credit or a loan and have an EMI obligation for them, it becomes much more crucial. Without a doubt, you do not want to burden your partner.

Financial disagreements may be a major turnoff for a newly established relationship. Couples breaking up because of their inability to manage financially challenging situations responsibly is more prevalent than we realise. Plan your emergency , including who has to be informed in case of emergencies, your chosen doctors and healthcare providers, and the credit card to be used for unanticipated costs. If you have made any sizable purchases using credit or a loan and have an EMI obligation for them, it becomes much more crucial. Without a doubt, you do not want to burden your partner. You must choose enough health insurance coverage to guarantee that any disease does not shatter your financial aspirations because healthcare inflation is 10%-15% compared to retail inflation, which is 6-7% every year. A health plan for newlyweds should include things like maternity coverage, no room rent cap or co-pay, pre-existing condition coverage, etc.

Working with couples to understand, accept, and value differences is frequently part of the last step of treatment. Therapists often use the example of someone being married to or connected with someone who is different from them, and then spending the rest of their marriage or relationship attempting to alter that person. Learning to tolerate differences is a necessary component of creating and maintaining respectful relationships. Regardless of whether this relates to ideals, goals, or temperament, partners must embrace the ways in which their spouse or partner is different. A crucial component of preserving a respectful relationship is tolerating, understanding, and even admiring how your spouse or partner differs from you. Working with couples to appreciate each other's strengths and the reality that differences do not have to be a danger to a partnership may go a long way toward assisting couples in achieving this tolerance. Respectful relationships entail questions about one another. They are interested in the other person's needs and feelings.

Neglecting emotional well-being will have a direct effect on both mental and physical well-being. Satisfying one's emotional demands, especially those of higher degree emotions, to the greatest extent feasible is the main goal of emotional management. The key to mastering relationships is to respect, facilitate, or assist others in achieving their goals. It has become more popular over the past two to three decades to minimise one's own and other people's emotions and dismiss them as insignificant. This pattern has accelerated due to ongoing acceptance and recurrences, which has resulted in the normalization of this warped emotional behavior.

In terms of how emotions are recognized, felt, reciprocated, satisfied, and controlled, most cultures are today seeing a worrisome level of standard decline. The operational ties that support partnerships are being weakened by this development. Relationships rely heavily on reciprocal satiation to survive, and when that ceases, they lose value and eventually end. Where have you come to if it is acceptable for children to disrespect their parents, if it is acceptable for parents to be unreliable in regards to their children's upbringing and education, if it is acceptable to distrust, if friendship has turned into opportunism, marriages into business deals, if sycophancy is referred to as professionalism, if violence is a workable solution, and if lying is a skill that is required to survive? Numerous additional criteria that your forebears established for a greater level of emotional intelligence in order to maintain relationships have also been diminished.

Lowering a society's emotional norms has unfavorable effects. That fury is already being felt by human civilization. Rarely do parents and young adults make eye contact or have deep, meaningful conversations. Workplaces suffer from a major lack of professionalism, as well as increased levels of disobedience, attrition, and ineptitude. Abuse of social media is on the increase, undermining differences of opinion and suppressing original thought. Already, respect between people is as uncommon as a white elephant. The trust has no takers. No longer considered a professional competency is careful communication. Human industry will quickly deteriorate and retreat into break-away anarchist and nomadic cults if human interactions are consistently undermined, undervalued, and disregarded.

One of the most crucial elements of every relationship is respect. It implies that you and your spouse are on equal footing. Everyone's voice is heard, and none is placed above the others. Couples who respect one another are free to be themselves, with their own interests, ideas, and feelings, without worrying about being rejected or facing retaliation from their spouse. Respect is essential to a successful marriage since it frequently takes precedence over love as the most vital quality. Given that it's hard to have one without the other, this makes sense. But respect may be challenging to measure, particularly as parents' roles and self-respect alter. So, what does respect in a loving relationship truly look like? One of the most crucial things partners can do for one another is validation. A fundamental desire for connection is met when your spouse can hear what you're saying, respect you, and comprehend you. As long as you can respect one another's perspectives, it is acceptable to disagree.

How can respect in a marriage be lost? Because of the demands and strains of daily life, respect can gradually dissolve. You or your spouse may become nasty and angry and take out your frustrations on them if you are under stress or going through personal difficulties. This may start a downward spiral in which spouses treat one another disrespectfully and negatively.This may start a downward spiral in which spouses treat one another disrespectfully and negatively. Similar to this, an inability to manage disagreements or differences can result in anger and irritation, which, if expressed negatively and unfairly, can set off the same cycle of unfavourable encounters and lead to the loss of respect. These are just a few examples of how respect in a marriage or relationship can deteriorate.

How can respect be created in a union or partnership? Respect is developed when you consistently: take into account and appreciate your spouse's thoughts and feelings; communicate with and treat your partner as you would like to be communicated with; and compromise and negotiate with your relationship.

Have you ever wondered why marriage is so difficult? Have issues in your marriage caused you to wonder whether your partnership will last? Most people find marriage difficult since it requires combining their lives and aspirations with another person's. Marriage issues following children or other significant changes can be difficult to handle and can cause resentment and feelings of disappointment. The cause of marital issues, however, is frequently negligence and complacent behaviour. If you handle the situation correctly and are willing to reflect, you can address these issues.

Going on dates with your partner after being married is one way to keep the romance alive. A partnership benefits from regular date evenings, but if things start to get dull and uninteresting, they should stop. Traditions like dinner and a movie are there for a purpose, but without a mix-up now and again, it may grow dull. You two can both enroll in a class that you both would appreciate, such as painting or cooking.

Without a filter, discuss your needs with one another. Communication is key in relationships. You must be open and honest in our communication, as well as listen carefully and without hesitation. Carrying grudges and resentments internally may have an impact on how satisfied you are with the relationship and with yourself. However, in order to achieve this, you must have empathy for your spouse and be able to understand why they are acting the way they are. When your spouse falls short of your expectations or the relationship is not progressing as you would like it to, you should let your partner know.

Take some more time to be apart. If you lived together and/or spent all of your time together, you would get weary of each other. Therefore, before you start to attribute your unhappiness to a lack of emotion or connection, consider taking some time apart. The fact that being around cheerful people makes you happy should not come as a surprise. Instead of relying on relationships to make your life better, focus on building a fulfilling and enjoyable life for yourself and whoever you are dating.

Married Indians reported that 93% of their unions were planned in a 2018 poll of more than 160,000 Indian homes. Only 3% of people reported having a "love marriage," and 2% said their union was "love-cum-arranged," which often means that the connection was arranged by the families before the couple decided to wed. The percentage hasn't changed much over time; it's still over 90% for young couples in their 20s, and 94% of octogenarians had an arranged marriage. In contrast, a few males approached her to chat during her first few days of college, and older female classmates escorted her to the restroom to have a discussion with her. They cautioned her not to talk to boys because it would damage her reputation. Everyone wants to be loved, but when you can't accept that you will occasionally disagree with your spouse, a problem might occur. In order to feel accepted and confident, you want to satisfy them.

When you make a persistent effort to win your partner's favor, you put your own integrity in jeopardy. You risk losing sight of the importance of your own judgment if you and your spouse always agree, no matter what. You can develop the habit of always siding with your lover. It's crucial that you don't constantly concur with them merely to maintain peace. You don't have to engage in conflict. You have the option of sensitively expressing your views.

You should view the other person in a marriage as an extension of yourself, like an arm or leg. One mind, one soul, two bodies. Therefore, you convert whatever your partner wants into your own desire. Consider your spouse's taste to be your own. When your tastes start diverging, conflict develops. You should start saying things like "Your joy is my pleasure" and "Your taste is my taste." I'm here for you, not "what can you do for me?"

It's crucial to keep in mind that: Both partners suffer when you enter into a relationship asking, "What can you do for me?" Each pair commits to the other in a good marriage: "I'm here for you, come what may, joyful times or terrible times!" Success and disappointment both occur in life sometimes. I'm with you in either situation. It might become monotonous to keep doing the same thing, and it can be hard to make adjustments in a secure relationship before it's too late. An occasional attempt at something novel may liven up a relationship.

Jealousy may ruin a marriage, particularly if the sentiments are unfounded. People that are jealous may become domineering and intrusive or irate and unaccepting. Consult a counsellor if you're experiencing jealousy to determine whether your sentiments are reasonable. Your potential attachment issue should be explored with a qualified counsellor. Many of the usual issues that arise in marriage can be avoided, rectified, or handled by utilising a variety of approaches and strategies.

Look at the most common marital problems that married people have, and discover effective solutions before your relationship suffers irreversible harm. Stress levels may increase depending on how it is handled and managed. Stress in a relationship needs to be managed because if it isn't, it will end badly. By having an open conversation with each other while being patient, you can try to find a solution. If chatting doesn't work, you might try engaging in stress-relieving activities like yoga or meditation. Most individuals find marriage difficult since it requires combining their lives and aspirations with another person's. Marriage issues following children or other significant changes can be difficult to handle and can cause anger and feelings of disappointment.

The cause of marital issues, however, is frequently negligence and complacent conduct. If you handle the situation correctly and are willing to reflect, you can address these issues. Many of the usual issues that arise in marriage may be prevented, rectified, or handled by employing a variety of approaches and strategies. Look at the most common marital difficulties that married people have, and discover effective solutions before your relationship suffers irreversible harm.

- One of the most prevalent marital issues in couples is infidelity. According to the most recent data, compared to 10% of women, roughly 20% of males who were asked acknowledged having an extramarital affair. Cheating and having emotional affairs are among them.
- According to new Cornell University research, couples who pool their finances have better levels of pleasure, harmony, and commitment in their committed relationships or marriage. The Journal of Personality and Social Psychology has published the findings. Researchers also found that relationships between couples with combined bank accounts tended to be stronger, and their interactions were more secure, stable, and happy. Marriage is more than simply two individuals joining forces to start a new life; it also entails sharing duties, including budgeting, expenditure sharing, investment planning, etc. One of the most important success indicators of a successful marriage is sound financial management and investment planning. The institution of marriage as a whole is witnessing

the rise of power couples, in which the husband and wife have substantial financial independence. Financial objectives can sometimes be quite individualised, which is why it's important to combine these goals and plan your financial future together. The secret is synergy. In addition to being a useful strategy for asset management and financial planning, married couples who enhance their financial future may also hold the secret to a happy and tranquil marriage.

- Dreams about money are never the same. Occasionally, one of your milestones will be exactly what your partner envisions. It is crucial that you get down, discuss your goals, make an assessment, and plan how you may meet halfway to create a financial future that works for the two of you. From the perspective of managing your daily family spending and budget appropriately, this recognition could also be required. Unexpected shocks are a part of life's continual change. In the present, this is more true than ever. In the midst of the dire macroeconomic and pandemic circumstances, health issues have gotten worse due to the uncertainty surrounding jobs and cashflows. These elements have only reinforced the need for the establishment of an emergency fund, which will make it easier to deal with difficult financial situations. Better results come faster.
- Do you and your spouse split the tasks fairly or equally? If not, it may seriously affect your marriage. To avoid becoming repetitive, communication is truly the key. Discuss the responsibilities with your spouse, including your feelings about them and how you might divide them between the two of you. A power imbalance in your partnership or marriage might cause issues down the road. Power might be material or simply related to how your relationships function. Talk about the power relationships in your relationship as a solution. While having departments that you both oversee is okay, it's crucial to have an equitable authority split.

- Do you cherish your spouse? Yes. But does your lover believe you love them? When there is a discrepancy in how two people display their love for one another, it might cause marriage trouble. Because you and your spouse do not have to express love in the same manner, this might cause misunderstandings. The answer is to recognise and comprehend your partner's displays of affection. Perhaps they go out of their way to do particular things for you to express their affection, but you are not aware of them since your viewpoint is different. When you recognise the same, be grateful to them. Share your thoughts, but also pay attention to what your spouse has to offer. And if they disagree with you, examine it, but don't let it make you feel intimidated.
- If you are in a relationship, it typically means that your values align with those of your spouse, albeit you may not always agree. Your partner can have values that are different from yours. Not that yours is incorrect or less realistic than theirs. It does not obligate you to alter them. Avoid becoming a doormat. It's dull to have a doormat. You are interesting because of your thoughts and beliefs. You know individuals that might come across as arrogant and domineering, and this is not what you're going for. Your core beliefs define who you are. Understanding your moral philosophy is crucial because it affects how you conduct your life.
- Mutual respect is a fairly straightforward idea. It implies that you show consideration and courtesy to your spouse or romantic partner. It entails avoiding harsh and disrespectful behaviour against one another, such as refraining from calling your partner or spouse names and refraining from insulting or demeaning them. Additionally, it entails that you do not mock, shun, or neglect your spouse. Mutual respect also entails giving your partner's thoughts, desires, and values substantial attention. Although it can seem easy, treating your spouse or partner with respect takes constant work. Respect is the existence of good actions as well as the absence of bad conduct. In particular, if you treat your spouse or partner with respect,

you will take into account and consult with them before making decisions that will have an impact on them, show an active interest in their lives (work, daily activities, and interests), and compromise and negotiate with them on significant issues that will have an impact on both of you and your family. Although by no means comprehensive, this list encapsulates the fundamentals of a respectful union or partnership.

- Respect takes effort to maintain over the course of a relationship.We are all human, and when someone treats us poorly, carelessly, or disrespectfully, we frequently have a tendency to return the kindness. This cycle of disdain for one another reinforces itself. The more one partner acts impolitely and carelessly, the more probable it is that the other spouse or partner will follow suit. Thus, disrespect can intensify to the point where the majority of encounters are marked by sarcastic, careless, blaming, criticising, and insulting behaviour. The lack of respect, meanwhile, is not often as clear. Insidious behaviours, such as neglecting their partner or replying to them indifferently, are also acceptable ways for partners or spouses to insult one another.
- Marriage should be a two-way street, but this isn't always the case. When it comes to domestic duties, child care, and emotional support, there are times when one spouse must provide somewhat more than the other, or when one or the other must step up and take on more. If they received sound counselling when their marriage began to experience significant difficulties (and remembered it), many couples could avoid divorce. The majority of couples should find these recommendations helpful.
- Couples frequently have contentious situations that lead to frequent disputes. Waiting before replying to something that has angered you helps lessen arguments. Discussing challenging topics while emotions are low may be preferable. Marriages experience ups and downs, as any married individual would attest. There are excellent, undesirable, and average timings. If

the positives, even slightly, exceed the negatives, a marriage is likely to succeed.It will get easier and you will feel more affectionate and connected to your spouse the more you attempt to enjoy the good and let the negative go.

- Pay at least as much attention to your marriage as you do to your interests. In their hobbies and interests outside of work, people invest a lot of time, money, and effort. But some give up and say it's pointless to continue trying when a marriage is making them feel miserable. Your marriage will benefit from reading books on communication, conflict resolution, and marriage. Even better is to have your partner read them.
- Support your partner's aspirations and ambitions. One partner in a happy marriage rejoices in the accomplishments of the other. Good partners encourage one another to accomplish goals. Goals like changing careers might be intimidating at times and require careful consideration. Work together. You should prioritise your relationship over everything else. Do you know the saying, "Familiarity breeds contempt?" Unfortunately, people frequently treat their wives worse than they do complete strangers. Become accustomed to treating your partner with the utmost respect.
- Have separate interests Ensure that you have a private area, and offer your partner one as well. While there is a lot of intimacy involved in marriage, it is not necessary to be attached at the hip. Look for activities that you and your partner will enjoy. A partnership is a marriage. If your hobbies are wholly dissimilar, you will gradually drift away. Discover things that you may enjoy together while keeping in mind that these preferences will certainly change over time.
- Don't worry over little details. Priorities should be set, just like in the working world. Pick your battles wisely and leave the other issues alone. Don't always believe that the grass is greener on the other side. Most people who leave their marriages for other partners discover the same issues elsewhere as well, and many of them regret not finding a solution in their first union.

- Put forth a lot of effort with your spouse to build financial stability. Making a successful joint enterprise on the financial front is one of the advantages of marriage. It will be one of the things that enables you to feel good about each other and the world as your financial stability increases. It will also serve as a gauge of how well you two have performed during your marriage. Give your spouse a compliment at least once per day. This promotes a healthy connection and is the proper course of action because your spouse is likely carrying out a lot of admirable deeds each day.
- Act as your partner's companion. Inform one another about the activities you are involved in, including your daily schedules at work and at home. Every day, the time you spend alone in the world is really important. Always share your day's experiences with one another at night. Be optimistic about your partner at all times. Everyone has had miscommunications and misunderstandings. If you don't like what your partner is doing, wait a little while and then attempt to figure out why. It's possible that your spouse intended to be positive rather than negative, and that your perception or assumption was incorrect.
- Occasionally, spoil your partner. Even if you don't particularly enjoy something your partner likes, you should occasionally offer it without being asked. It can be something modest, like a date to the movies, a ride to somewhere your spouse enjoys going, or perhaps a favourite shopping item. Respect one another's contributions to the marriage. Marriages frequently end in divorce due to perceived discrepancies in each party's degree of participation. Recognize the contributions made by the other person, whether they are monetary or emotional.
- Avoid arguing with your partner regarding the kids. Conflicts over children can seriously damage a marriage. Have your conversations offline to prevent your kids from learning that you disagree. If necessary, seek expert guidance to help you coordinate and respect your many viewpoints.Try not to criticise your spouse in front of friends and family. Long after the issue

or argument was handled, the listener will remember one complaint from a difficult moment in your marriage. If you need to discuss your marriage with someone, find a neutral professional.

- Many marriages end in affairs. Be honest with everyone and quit the marriage first if you are unable to resist someone outside of your marriage. Get together with mutual friends. It is sometimes quite beneficial for a marriage to pursue outside connections with single people or other couples. The length of a marriage makes terrible things inevitable. Every couple, including you, makes errors and occasionally mistreats each other. You must have the capacity to forget your spouse's transgressions against you and move on. The next time, keep it in mind since you might need to ask for forgiveness.

On a lighter note, marriage is similar to a video game. It is easy at first, gets tougher as you go along, and finally you go online and find a method to cheat.

NINE

MAXIMISE HAPPINESS BY MINIMISING CONFLICTS

PRINCIPLE-IX

"When both you and your spouse try to improve things, marriages endure the test of time. And when you encounter difficulties, you are tested the most. You have already won half the battle if you can overcome the challenges as a group. "
- Dr. Amit Das

Never choose a partner you can live with; instead, choose someone you can't live without.

Looking for marital happiness? Every married couple wants to live happily and peacefully. Everyone imagines their ideal marriage to be one that is full of joy, love, caring, trust, laughter, and chuckles. However, contentment in life may continue to elude some people, leading them to search for the formula for a happy marriage. Despite the fact that everyone who is married wants to be content and have a calm life, that is true, right? In order to discover joy and satisfaction in their lives, couples make trips to monks' and other monasteries, temples, churches, and other locations. But they overlook the fact that there are more factors that play a role in a happy marriage. When both partners put up effort, make concessions, and comprehend one another, marriages remain joyful. As a result, one should always seek happiness in their marriage. You wish to have a happy marriage as a married couple. The key to a good marriage, though, remains elusive, leading you to search for it. Marriages may be happy with work and cooperation. The happiness in your married life may be unlocked by using the following keys to a successful marriage:

Marriage is unique because it requires two people to share and strengthen their love while also learning to accept and live with one another's shortcomings.

It's because the degree of connection and your own levels of satisfaction determine how happy you are as a couple. You marry someone because you love them, and you undoubtedly want to live happily ever after. But even if you're content, you can't make your spouse genuinely content if that contentment doesn't originate from inside. You can express your happiness to your spouse, but you can not force it upon him or her or attempt to control it. Since marriage involves a partnership, the couples must be on the same page. They wouldn't be content if there was no comradery between the pair. togetherness. As a result, happiness in a marriage can only be found if both you and your spouse are truly content within and enjoy doing things together.

Instead of dwelling on the reasons why you are unhappy in your marriage or relationship or what your partner has done wrong, consider how you can improve the way you handle your marriage and relationship. Not just your spouse but also your way of life has to change if you believe that your marriage or relationship is unsatisfactory or that you are miserable and in the wrong partnership. If you really want to be happy in a marriage or relationship, do what makes you feel good from within. However, that doesn't imply you should make your partner miserable or unhappy.

As you can see, pleasure is found in those priceless moments spent together without any expectations. Basically, staying true to who you are in marriage is the best way to find happiness. And you don't allow your ego to get in the way of being genuinely open to the other person. You choose to live with and love your spouse because you genuinely care about them. By focusing on the things that truly matter and ignoring or letting go of the ones that don't, you have the opportunity to discover happiness. There are many twists and turns in life. However, if you live in a marriage and look for companionship in one another, you may make your trip through life meaningful.

You should be aware that frequent marital issues like these are what make marriages difficult. Now that you are aware of the most frequent marital issues, it is crucial to pinpoint their root causes as well. The following are reasons for marital issues:

- First and foremost, listen to your companion. A couple's activity such as dancing or hiking might help you pay attention to each other in a novel and invigorating way. You may be able to filter out background noise and truly concentrate on each other.
- Lack of communication or misunderstanding is one of the most frequent reasons for marital issues. You are more prone to experiencing marital issues if you are not clear about your sentiments, limits, and expectations in your marriage.
- Having unclear expectations about your relationship, your marriage, or how things will function between the two of you can potentially cause problems in your marriage.
- It could lead to marital issues if you and your spouse step outside of the relationship and talk about every facet of it with your parents, kids, friends, or even siblings. Although certain issues should be kept private between the two of you, your relationship

does not have to be kept secret.

- If you and your partner never talk about the issues you are facing, it might lead to a lot of marital strife. If you and your spouse lie to one another or withhold information from one another, it may lead to marital issues.
- One-night stands, physical infidelity, online connections, and both long-term and short-term encounters are further examples of adultery. Infidelity arises in a relationship for a variety of reasons; it is a prevalent issue for which many couples are unable to come up with a solution.
- When the bond between you and your partner is weak, infidelity can occur and can erode trust. According to research, the three most effective strategies to prevent infidelity in a relationship are to establish a solid emotional connection, engage in sexual closeness, and respect boundaries.
- In a long-term partnership, physical closeness is essential, but it's also the main source of sexual problems, which are among the most prevalent marital issues ever. For a variety of reasons, sexual issues in a relationship can arise, setting the stage for later marital issues. According to studies, sexual compatibility and sexual pleasure were recognised as the most important factors in predicting a couple's contentment with their relationship.
- The key to overcoming any type of sexual incompatibility is communication and maintaining an open mind. It can rebuild the necessary emotional and physical bonds for healthy sexual intimacy.
- Within a marriage, there will undoubtedly be conflicts and differences, but some of these differences, like fundamental ideas and ideals, are too important to overlook. Each partner may practise a different faith from one another.
- In other cases, a spouse's sexual preferences may be the cause of a sexual issue. It's possible that one partner in a relationship prefers different sexual activities than the other, which makes the other partner uncomfortable. The emotional chasm may

result from a difference in values, among other typical marital issues.

- Nothing compares to having a good start on your long-term objectives. Only in the last several years has the magic of compounding returns begun to work, and the longer the tenure, the higher the corpus will be. It is also simpler to accomplish your objectives without any difficulties. Your viewpoint matters. It is worth it. It is equally valid for you and your partner. It is simple to assume that your spouse will have better concepts, ideas, or viewpoints.
- It is a good idea to be open to new ideas since they could have more expertise or experience than you have in a certain field, and their perspectives might help you form your own. But if you have opinions, don't be hesitant to voice them, even if you feel that your partner's perspective is more valuable. If your spouse has a different opinion than you, especially if they are self-assured, you can assume that they must be correct and you are mistaken. That is not the situation.
- As you might have anticipated, this might result in serious issues if one spouse grows weary of attending various places of worship or engaging in other activities separately. These marital issues are common in intercultural unions. Core values are among the other variations. These include the methods used to raise children and the lessons they learned as youngsters, such as the meaning of good and wrong.
- There is a lot of space for disagreement and conflict inside the partnership because no two people grow up with the same belief systems, beliefs, or ambitions. Conflicts resulting from disparate ideals may only be resolved via compromise and discussion. The best course of action in situations where compromise is impossible is to show understanding and accept that there will be disagreement.
- When it comes to relationships, many people fail to take their life phases into account. Marriage problems can occasionally arise only from the fact that both partners have outgrown one

another and desire different things in life. Whether there is an older man and a younger woman or an older woman and a younger guy, growing apart over time is a problem that frequently affects married couples. Couples may no longer be as compatible as they once were, as personalities change with time. This typical marital issue affects couples who are in different stages of life and have varied ages.

- Take regular stock of your relationship to make sure you and your spouse continue to grow closer rather than further away. Try to embrace and enjoy the various changes that life will bring to each of you, both separately and together. A different thing to attempt is a sport. Try to take up new interests that will enable you to reconnect with one another and strengthen your relationship.
- Traumatic events present couples with additional obstacles in their marriage. Couples may also have issues related to traumatic events. Many terrible incidents change people's lives. Some married couples experience trouble as a result of these traumatic events because one partner lacks the necessary skills to deal with the circumstances. Because the other spouse is in the hospital or on bed rest, one spouse might not know how to operate without the other. In some cases, one spouse can need 24-hour care, making the other spouse their only source of support.
- Sometimes the demands and responsibilities become too much to handle, causing the relationship to deteriorate until it is completely over. Then take a break! Even if it can sound selfless, spending some time with yourself will help your relationship. A therapist can support you or your spouse through any traumatic event and equip you with the skills you need to overcome these obstacles. Most couples will experience stress as a marital issue at some point throughout their partnership. Financial, family, emotional, and physical conditions are just a few of the many circumstances that can lead to stress in relationships and other situations.

- Financial difficulties may result from a spouse losing their job or getting fired. Children, issues with their relatives, and the family of the spouse can all cause family stress. There are several factors that cause stress. Stress levels may increase depending on how it is handled and controlled. Do not be misled into thinking that married couples do not encounter their fair share of problems and difficulties since marriage is frequently perceived as the "happily ever after" period of relationships.
- You may support and encourage your spouse to step outside of their comfort zone and do new things in order to realise their goals and confront their anxieties when you have a better understanding of them. These little details could consist of: preparing meals together, demonstrating interest in the small elements of one another's life and providing for one another's needs while ill; arranging a date night; and surprising each other at work.
- While some typical marital issues are simple to fix, others may be more challenging and even signify the beginning of the end of a marriage. Relationship problems can result from a variety of factors, including divergent values, personality characteristics, and communication preferences. Low self-esteem in one or both spouses, ongoing anxiety or depression, a lack of intimacy, feeling heard, and relational confidence are all indicators of a failed marriage.
- Stress in a relationship needs to be managed because if it isn't, it will end badly. By having an open conversation with each other while being patient, you may try to find a solution. If chatting doesn't work, you could try engaging in stress-relieving activities like yoga or meditation. One spouse frequently tries to modify their spouse after the couple gets married. Trying to modify your spouse is a personal invasion; whether it's their sense of style or their core values, the affected spouse will feel insulted, wounded, or even enraged when it occurs.
- Overstepping a person's personal boundaries frequently occurs on purpose and with a goal in mind. Retaliation or retreat from

the attacked spouse is likely to be the outcome of this kind of behaviour since it tramples on the basic concept of mutual respect. It therefore makes it challenging for partners to express their love, care, and openness to one another. Additionally, it is possible to unknowingly cross personal boundaries, particularly if you are really attempting to assist your partner.

- Even though the terms "talking" and "communicating" are sometimes used synonymously, it's crucial to realise that they are very different from one another. Speaking involves imparting information without expecting a reaction, which gives an opportunity for griping and criticism. However, communication is a vocal and nonverbal information exchange that necessitates a reaction. It is concentrated on a connection between individuals where it is safe to openly exchange thoughts and information without fear of rejection since communication requires more than one person. When partners don't communicate well with one another, it's easy for them to develop bad communication habits. Even worse, if poor communication skills are not addressed, they may lead to more significant problems.While having sex may seem like a minor aspect of marriage, it's actually uncommon to have a happy relationship without it.
- A serious yet underappreciated marriage issue is boredom. Some couples eventually become tired of each other. They could grow weary of the events that take place in the relationship. It comes down to boredom in this case, because the relationship has grown boring due to its predictability. Take an unusual action as a solution.To end the boredom in your relationship, whether it be in the bedroom or other aspects of life. Watch your relationship change when you pleasantly surprise your lover with a present, an unexpected idea, or a novel sexual action.
- Another typical marital issue that destabilises marriages is jealousy. It can be difficult to be with them and around them if your partner is extremely possessive. As long as it is not excessively jealous, jealousy can be somewhat appropriate in any

relationship. Such people will be nosy; they may ask who you are on the phone with, why, how, and how long you have known them. A relationship that is extremely stressed will eventually end because of an overly jealous spouse. The only way to effectively deal with insecurity is via self-reflection, which is the only cure for extreme jealousy. If you find it difficult to do this on your own, a psychologist can assist you or your spouse in understanding the causes of your jealousy and how to reduce it.

- When spouses go too far in trying to influence their partner's beliefs, it can lead to this prevalent relationship issue. Such a disrespect for your partner's boundaries can occur unintentionally, but the severity of the retribution from the spouse who is being assaulted is usually subdued over time. Learn to accept your partner's boundaries and stop pressuring them to make changes as well as simply loving them. If you have trouble embracing some aspects of your relationship, try to keep in mind that both of you fell in love with them for who they are.
- Even if you have known someone for a long time, a little change in facial expression or any other kind of body language can lead to misunderstandings because communication comprises both verbal and non-verbal indicators. Men and women interact extremely differently and are prone to developing bad communication habits. The purity of marriage is unquestionably in jeopardy if such marital or relationship problems are allowed to fester. Negative communication habits can develop, and the only way to break them is to consciously work to change them. You can gradually pick up effective communication skills that benefit both the relationship and the people involved.
- Every marriage eventually encounters the "lack of attention" problem when a spouse, whether on purpose or accidentally, diverts their focus to other areas of their lives. Lack of focus People are social animals that actively seek out the attention of others, particularly those who are close to them. Lack of focus alters the dynamics of a marriage, causing one or both partners

to overreact and act out. If this marital issue is not resolved properly, it might become out of hand.

- Money may end a marriage more quickly than anything else. You will experience money issues in your marriage, whether you create a joint account or manage your funds independently. It's critical to have open conversations about any financial concerns in a marriage. Couples should carefully address their financial issues as they might be touchy. Create a strategy that satisfies your mutual financial objectives. Also, if someone deviates from the plan, make an effort to ensure that the rationale is fully stated.
- Lack of appreciation for, acknowledgment of, and thankfulness for your spouse's contribution to your relationship. Lack of appreciation for, acknowledgment of, and thankfulness for your spouse's contribution to your relationship. Your relationship may suffer if you're unable to show your partner appreciation. Make an effort to value all that your partner brings to the table. To express your gratitude, leave them a surprise letter, send them flowers, or treat them to a spa day. Make an effort to tell your partner if you feel underappreciated in the relationship. Express your thoughts and need for change without placing blame on them or making them feel cornered.
- As a result of the tremendous rise in our involvement and fixation with technology and social media, we are becoming farther away from constructive face-to-face connection. The social internet is quickly becoming a threat to marriage and family. Because of your candour with them, they may recognise their error and make changes.You are losing yourselves in a virtual world and forgetting to love those and things around you. Such preoccupation has quickly emerged as a typical marital issue. Dedicate a day or an hour each day to being technology-free for you and your partner. To try and focus on each other without interruption, keep your phones and other electronics out of the room.

- This frequent marital conflict can destroy your union from the inside out, giving you little chance to mend your bonds. The concept of trust in a marriage is still extremely traditional, and when doubt begins to creep into a partnership, it may often place too much strain on a marriage. Open conversation can aid a couple in understanding the causes of their mistrust and how to address them, with the support of a therapist. To assist you in learning to trust one another, the therapist could also recommend certain exercises that foster trust.
- Even though selfishness is a common marital issue, it may be effectively resolved by making little adjustments to your attitude toward your spouse. Integrating your life with that of the other person and their priorities is a huge aspect of being in a relationship. This adjustment can be challenging for couples since there may be conflicts between personal and group objectives. The only thing that can stop selfish conduct is empathy. Make it a practise to be thoughtful of others and try to comprehend one another's viewpoints. Talk to your spouse openly and honestly if your own aims conflict with those of your relationship.
- The foundation of an unhealthy relationship can be laid by keeping score of fights won and lost inside a relationship. It would fuel hatred and make you always desire to settle the score. The emphasis shifts from supporting one another to gaining the upper hand. Relationships are not the place to keep score in sports. By learning not to keep track of who won arguments and conflicts, you may learn to deal with marital issues. Let go of the minor conflicts so you can concentrate on the broader picture.
- Sadly, a typical marital issue is losing your temper, yelling or screaming in fury, and hurting yourself or your partner physically. An outburst at your loved ones may be quite damaging to a relationship when you are under rising stress for both internal and external reasons and are in a fit of rage. If you suffer from anger, think about speaking with a counsellor to learn coping mechanisms that can help you keep your anger

under control so it doesn't interfere with your relationships. Alternatively, you might begin by counting to 10 before uttering any hurtful comments that could damage your relationship. A common response when anger takes over in a marriage is to seek revenge or retaliation from your spouse. Let go of the minor conflicts you may have had to compromise on and concentrate on the broader issue.

- It's not just adultery or selfishness that constitutes lying as a typical marital issue; it also includes telling white lies about mundane matters. These falsehoods are frequently used to maintain your dignity and prevent your partner from taking the initiative. Marriage issues arise when partners lie to one another about challenges or issues they may be experiencing at work or in other social settings. When things spiral out of control, a marriage can be seriously destroyed. Consider the reasons why you or your partner feel pressured to tell lies rather than the truth. You can only try to stop the lying and dishonesty in your relationship when you fully comprehend and take care of these causes. We all acknowledge that marriage is a commitment that lasts a lifetime, yet we seldom take the time to get to know our spouses before we tie the knot. Without even considering whether or not you have the same goals in life, you take your ideals of the ideal marriage from the stories you have heard or from the individuals you know.
- As terrible as it may be, it's typical for couples to lose emotional connections with one another after marriage. When this occurs, it's possible that at least one partner will have their needs unfulfilled and may start seeking fulfilment elsewhere. This is the point at which emotional "infidelity" has the potential to enter a marriage. Since emotional adultery involves more than sex and involves connecting with another person deeply, some individuals believe it to be worse than physical infidelity. Couples need to be clear about what they both mean by cheating in order to prevent infidelity of any form. Getting on the same page will reduce the likelihood that partners will allow infidelity to occur.

At first, couples may not feel the same way about what constitutes cheating and what doesn't. Couples should continue to support one another's emotional needs since when they are satisfied, they won't be as interested in seeking them out elsewhere. When this occurs, it's normal for married individuals to overreact, which is a mistake since it essentially tells their partner they can't live without them. When couples get closer, their bank accounts frequently increase as well. Even married couples who want to keep their funds apart still have financial difficulties, although this may not always be the case.

- A couple's differences over their relationship's prospects for the future leave a lot of potential for the development of false expectations.There is a lot of potential for the development of irrational expectations from our spouse when there is a mismatch between a couple's perspectives on the direction of their relationship. Just let it go! Accept reality and be grateful for all the relationships you have. Recognise that no relationship can live up to your expectations and that they are unreal. Even when a relationship is going well, expectations may still create a norm.
- The development of romantic feelings for someone other than one's partner, however, is referred to as emotional adultery. Since having affections for someone else might harm your marriage or relationship, emotional infidelity can potentially develop into a marital issue. Self-assessment if you begin to sense a connection with someone else. Look within to see what these emotions signify.
- When these expectations are not met, bitterness, disillusionment, and the marriage are all pushed in a direction from which there may be no turning back. While criticising your spouse for certain aspects of their behaviour is acceptable, it might not be a good idea to push them too far or cross any limits they have established. If not resolved right away, this might cause problems in your marriage. Talk about limits as a solution. If you desire a night out with your pals every two weeks, let your spouse know. If they don't comprehend the idea of boundaries,

explain it to them. Encourage children to establish sound limits for themselves as well. Likewise, respect their bounds.

- Because trust is the basic foundation of love, a happy marriage is impossible without it. A spouse's infidelity, deceit, or breach of a vow can be very damaging to the marriage. In a marriage, when one partner has deceived the other, it can be difficult to rebuild trust. Both partners must be dedicated to repairing the marriage in order to get past the problem. This is true if you want to resolve your marital issues. The deceived spouse will continue to feel wounded, angry, and suspicious if the issues are not resolved.
- It might be challenging to resist becoming enamoured with electronic devices in a society that is primarily controlled by technology. Because of this, an increasing number of couples claim that their partner's fascination with technology is causing problems in their marriages. Let's imagine, for instance, that a woman becomes so engrossed in her smartphone that she texts her friends at the dinner table rather than conversing with her husband. Perhaps a husband is glued to his iPad and just wants to play games and check Facebook after supper. These circumstances may take the place of constructive interaction and even intimacy. These may seem strange, yet they are actual problems.
- It won't take long for the ignored spouse to begin to feel worthless and unwanted if one spouse constantly prioritises their own needs and wants over those of the other. When a couple gets married, they make the commitment to love one another through good and bad times, and a part of that commitment is to refrain from being selfish. Although it might seem simple enough, the green-eyed monster can take many cunning forms. Selfishness may be harsh, manipulative, possessive, jealous, and domineering at its worst. It might be detected in less severe versions as a lack of regard and concern. Even though it's common for married couples to occasionally become upset with one another, it's crucial that both partners

respond correctly when these circumstances happen. Couples should address the matter at hand (remain on topic), maintain composure, and take into account one another's sentiments rather than react violently with outbursts or fits of wrath. Couples should also practise active listening, honest opinion-expression, and avoidance of defensiveness.

On a lighter note, any husband who asserts that his wife and he are "fully equal partners" is either referring to a legal company or a game of bridge.

TEN

GIVE YOUR SPOUSE A SECOND CHANCE

PRINCIPLE-X

"Everyone has a past. I have mine, you have yours, and we all have ours. No matter what it takes, I will prove to you that our past, no matter how hurtful, didn't ruin the future we could have had. " -Melissa Foster.

You might not do everything right the first time, so it's crucial to try things again.

If your expectations aren't met, you could become unhappy, and in a marriage or relationship, unmet expectations frequently result in resentment. A marriage or relationship may end if these grudges are not cleared up or are not expressed. Yes, having fewer expectations is beneficial, but this is unrealistic since it means stifling your own aspirations. Living in the now and finding satisfaction in those times while having fewer expectations for the future is beneficial. Remember that you must find solutions to your issues promptly if there is a meltdown or fight! Recognize the issue and work to develop solutions so that it doesn't happen again. Move on to enjoy a happy married life by forgiving and forgetting.

Your partner could have told you about their previous relationships or romantic exploits. On the outside, you could appear unaffected, but when you're by yourself, you might look into your "ex's" internet actions. You could begin to feel envious and get fixated on them, constantly following them to learn more about them and see whether they're in contact with your spouse. Your relationship will suffer from this compulsive conduct. Perhaps you are content with your existing companion. However, receiving a message from an ex on your messenger might bring back bad emotions and entice you to start dating again. Even if you don't mean any harm, your spouse can feel threatened by the fact that you are still in touch with someone with whom you had a strong relationship, which might lead to conflict between you two. It is better to avoid letting the past influence the present.

Finding marital bliss is not difficult if you are ready to put in the effort. Maintain open lines of communication and improve your listening skills. Don't hold things in since ineffective communication can cause issues in relationships. Instead of disclosing your issues to strangers, speak out about them. Don't always express your needs, wishes, or feelings. Be honest with your spouse and learn to listen to what they want. When you believe that your partner is upsetting or making you sad, respond appropriately. Talk that may make things worse should be avoided. Avoid stonewalling, where one party just ignores or leaves the other partner for a while while remaining silent and cutting off communication. Stonewalling frequently results in rage and frustration, which makes marital issues worse.

If you believe that your marriage is having a difficult time, don't just leave it. Rather, face it courageously. If you want to save my marriage, try to identify the source of the issue before attempting to solve it. Take a look at what's upsetting you or straining your marriage. There is undoubtedly a fix for every issue. Avoid giving up on it so quickly and readily. Maybe you're concentrating on the issue too much, which is making you more anxious. It would be better for you if you started concentrating on other significant things, such as your spouse's positive traits. Your mental health might be harmed by obsessions! Undoubtedly, the instant you changed your attention, you would discover the solution to the question of "how to preserve your marriage by yourself."

Openness and flexibility are necessary for growth during the course of a marriage. For those of faith, it also means being aware of the enigmatic ways in which the Holy Spirit operates. Faith calls for trust and submission, but modern culture seeks answers and assurance. God extends the offer to enter into marriage and provides the means to do so. Even if we cannot see the complete path and its destination, God provides us enough clarity to proceed with the next few steps.

Try to demonstrate to your spouse that you are capable of handling marital issues with confidence and a positive outlook. False promises and little effort might cause your spouse to have doubts about your relationship. Make sure that whatever was lacking on your side gets done by taking charge of your relationship. It demonstrates how crucial it is for you to understand how to preserve your marriage, and working on this connection will also inspire your partner.

When it comes to everything, from doing chores to talking, feeling unappreciated might make someone doubt whether they should even attempt it. Regularly expressing your gratitude for them and the things they do, such as helping around the house, watching the kids, or working hard every day, is crucial for saving a marriage. It will increase their self-esteem and make them feel loved and appreciated, which will make them feel good about the marriage.

Talking about money with your spouse may be uncomfortable and frustrating, particularly if the two of you have different spending patterns or approaches to managing your finances. It's typical for the debate to shift away from money and into personal values and habits in these kinds of tense circumstances. For instance, when one partner is under financial pressure, they may be less tolerant and more irritable overall, which puts a burden on both of them. Without realising it, they could even argue with their partner on irrelevant issues. Conflict is prone to increase when appreciation between married spouses declines. Finding a balance between personal interests and being a devoted partner is crucial since, in these circumstances, couples may even start to feel more like roommates than lovers.

Identify the areas where you and your spouse are having trouble, and then focus on finding solutions that will satisfy both of you. It's a proactive way to discover "how to preserve your marriage on your own." Your relationship's issues won't go away by themselves. You must acknowledge the differences and come up with a strategy to allay your worries. Your efforts will have purpose and drive as a result. Try to lend a helping hand to your spouse with everything they are attempting to complete, whether it be domestic duties or other obligations. Before they have a chance to feel the weight of what is on their shoulders, offer your assistance. These kind deeds will lighten and cheer up your partner's mood. Additionally, they will flourish in happiness under the light of your thoughtfulness and care.

As long as they plan their calendars to make time for one another, it's quite okay (and even recommended) for couples to have their own individual interests and objectives. Those formerly modest but heartfelt surprise acts of kindness lose their allure and turn into a chore rather than a choice when they start to be anticipated. It's crucial to continue praising your spouse for the things you've both accomplished, whether you've been married for a year or ten years.

The easiest way to understand marriage is to think of it as a set of phases that most couples go through as they spend the rest of their lives together. Although each of these seven stages of marriage is unique and somewhat independent from the others, they are all interrelated. Each pair can adapt to the changes more easily if they are prepared and know what to anticipate. The phases of marriage that many married couples experience nowadays are described here.

The "honeymoon" period of marriage begins immediately following the wedding and lasts for the next few months, perhaps extending as long as a year or two. It is universally accepted as romantic, emotional, and idealistic. The phrase "the honeymoon's over" is not just a catchphrase! As the first stage of marriage concludes, the second one begins; it may do so gradually or abruptly, depending on the events impacting the bride, the husband, and their future together.

Power battles may break out after the first years or so when each spouse stakes out their territory and establishes their lines of defence. The spouse may only be a small part of how each partner reinvents themselves at this point of the marriage when they start to understand they married someone with more faults than virtues.

Show your selected partner love and support. Show your chosen partner love and support. Both you and your partner crave approval. You may discuss your shared aims and goals with your partner. Analyze whether you both have emotional appreciation and validation for the connection. Perhaps now is the appropriate moment to discuss all of these issues, as you likely did at the start of your relationship.

It would be wise to realise that your difficulties won't magically disappear if you are considering divorcing. It would be better if you exercised patience and trust. The connection was harmed over time, and healing it will take time as well. There is no quick fix. To save your relationship, make a commitment to repair the harm you both have done and continually strive toward that goal.

If you want to save your relationship, you both need to be more empathic.Putting yourself in your partner's position, considering their struggles, and coming up with solutions might be beneficial. Your connection may improve as a result of your ability to empathise. You have to realise that competition is unnecessary. You can come up with a solution that meets both of your demands. Different people have different ways of showing their affection. Men and women yearn for the same thing: to be valued. Even though it is so easy to let your spouse know you appreciate them, many people choose not to.

Asking your spouse about their day, wants, desires, challenges, and pleasures is a significant approach to changing your marriage. They will feel heard, appreciated, and valued as a result of it. They'll understand how much you value them, which will make your marriage stronger. People talk to you when you experience such acute melancholy, and most of the time they make unpleasant remarks or engage in bad conversation. All those disparaging remarks about your partner and your union might tarnish your relationship. Make certain that none of you are associated with such people. It would also be ideal if you both refrained from criticising one another. Respect the other person as you would like to be treated.

Keep your cool and cooperate with your spouse, even when things are difficult or not going as planned. There are several occasions in a marriage where you may demonstrate your compassion and love for others. Be patient and recognise that you and your spouse are both under stress, so it may take some time to resolve the situation and meet your requirements. Why is it crucial to keep your marriage intact? You might want to grasp the reasons why it is crucial to put in a lot of effort to save a marriage before asking yourself, "How to save my marriage by myself."

Moving forward the couple may experience peaceful moments during their second or third decade of marriage after enduring boredom, conflict, and temptation thus far. Suddenly, they have another chance to rediscover one another. This is a wonderful chance for them to refocus on each other rather than juggling kids, jobs, and difficulties that come with marriage when children grow up and leave for college and one or both couples settle into fulfilling employment.

Make an investment of time and effort. Any kind of connection, even a marriage, needs ongoing care. To generate a strong return on investment as a pair, you must invest your time, energy, and money, among other things. Do not hesitate to seek out outside, qualified assistance.The secret to every marriage's sustainability is consistent investment. When defending a relationship, one must be willing to explore new avenues for getting to know their partner and their connection. Reading more about how to save your marriage and using the advice you learn from professionals to improve your marriage is one way to do this. However, you shouldn't be scared to seek outside marital assistance, particularly when objective third parties that are skilled in actively resolving marital issues can be able to greatly assist you. Outside assistance might provide the boost you need if you and your spouse find it difficult to communicate and work through challenges as a married pair.

Couples that are strong and dedicated will find a way to endure the crisis. Sadly, some people may be left behind as their marriages fail. After a few decades, the husband and wife come to the realisation that they have successfully maintained their marriage at this point, and they are happy to continue doing so for the remainder of their lives. Some couples may choose to do this by just reflecting on their earlier years of marriage and feeling grateful they had each other through both good and terrible times. It's possible that you won't go through each stage of marriage in the same sequence. Or perhaps you'll encounter items that aren't on this list. The essential issue is that few marriages function continuously on one level for the length of two people's whole lives after deciding to be married. There are many different situations that people go through that might affect how they feel about their partner.

There are good and terrible periods in every marriage, but there are also many joyful ones. Therefore, no marriage is perfect. Do you not enjoy your marriage? Happiness is a condition of mind, whether it be in your marriage, family, friends, or any other connection. You will experience happiness when you desire it. Isn't that true? Nothing, though, can truly make you happy if you can find reasons to be unhappy. I don't claim to have all the answers for making a marriage work, but I have shared the techniques or strategies that have benefited me in the past and continue to do so.

Keep in mind that you must work on your marriage or any other relationship in order to achieve happiness. Knowing why love hurts and what threatens your marriage might help you learn to make apologies. When anything goes wrong, you should pause and consider what you might change to improve your marriage, maybe by making some compromises.The benefits of a good marriage on your health and career make it all worthwhile.

In the early stages of a relationship, couples frequently speak freely and extensively. They go out of their way to surprise and satisfy each other and appear to anticipate each other's wants and desires. Couples start to feel very strongly like "we." When observed at all, individual differences are downplayed, and couples are highly tolerant. There is much joy, enthusiasm, pleasure, and optimism. Each partner displays and brings forth their finest self. Life appears to be abundant and hopeful. It's a season of romance and dream-sharing. Couples' prayers at this point are frequently ones of appreciation and adoration. God seems to be quite responsive and nearby. This is a moment to appreciate and remember.

Remember how you promised to love and respect your spouse forever when you said "I do"? It should come as no surprise that the majority of marriages end within the first five years, or even sooner. Others may be seen drowning the moment the first huge wave hits their marital boat, while some of the couples manage to make it through the difficult times. Everyone agrees that the honeymoon stage in the majority of Indian marriages does indeed have a shelf life, but that doesn't mean you should let your relationship deteriorate because things aren't working out the way you had hoped.

Through improved communication, honesty, and trust, couples can go past the previous stage. They should ideally find and forge a new bond. They get better insight into one another's advantages and weaknesses. Instead of acting out their concerns, they learn to recognise them and talk about them. They interpret their concerns into calls for change rather than passing judgement or assigning blame to their spouse.

Fighting, shouting, yelling, and hurling insults at each other doesn't solve anything. If you can't put away your fighting gloves, put away your fighting words, and tackle the issues with a deliberate conversation rather than a battle, you can't restore your shattered marriage. It is not the solution to the question of "How to make a marriage work?" to rant at your spouse about your issues. The goal is to be able to reasonedly debate with them as a group. This does not imply that you should suppress your feelings. After all, having a marriage issue will inevitably make you both emotional. It simply implies that you should promote conversation rather than conflict.

In a new light, partners view each other as both talented and fallible, just as they do. Compassion and empathy grow. They discover new ways to value and respect one another and stop taking one another for granted. They achieve a new equilibrium between closeness and independence, between being alone and with others. Their minds enlarge and become more inclusive. The partnership experiences a rebirth of optimism and vitality.

Couples frequently progress to a more sincere and developed connection with God as a result of prayer's emphasis on appreciation and thanksgiving. Additional life cycle stages, each with their own benefits and difficulties, will be experienced by many couples. Similar to marriage, starting a family will bring out the best and worst traits, as well as the strengths and weaknesses of the parents. It offers an additional chance to learn about teamwork and cooperation, how to handle disagreements and disputes, and how to pause to make a decision. Parenting is a spiritual journey that involves the development of both the parents and the children.

Similar to marriage, it will present several possibilities for giving up control, dying to oneself, letting go, and grieving. Sickness, unemployment, other financial difficulties, retirement, and relationship death are further life cycle obstacles. Many couples have to let go of the younger generation in order to care for the elderly.

We have all made errors at some point in our lives, but if everything went wrong afterward, we wouldn't be inspired to attempt anything new. Just consider the occasions that life or other people have given you a second opportunity. You are by no means ever compelled to offer someone else another chance. It requires work on the part of both the girl and the guy to rekindle the love and joy in a relationship. To give your relationship a fresh start, you must give it all you have. The following are a few short and simple suggestions to help you rekindle your marriage. New beginnings are inherently thrilling, hopeful, a little frightening, and brimming with anticipation.

The intriguing thing is that fresh starts don't often include meeting new people. For people still caught up in dull relationships, dysfunctional relationships, unpleasant relationships, turbulent relationships, or simply relationships that seem to be finished, new beginnings can be a fresh start.

In "dead marriages" and "disconnected relationships," so many individuals experience the weight of their situation and are overcome with desire and longing for "what was" or "I wish it could be different." Of course, it can! Amazing fresh beginnings only materialise when you pinpoint the true issue and work to discover answers. Doing the same thing over and over again and expecting different outcomes is said to be being stupid. New beginnings require constructive change.

Do you frequently complain? Have you ever had a good time with your partner? Would you want to return home to a person who is similar to you? "No The responses to these inquiries may astound you and reveal what you may be doing to harm your marriage.You should attempt to spend time doing things that make you happy, even if life isn't always fun and games and there are important things to take care of. Work on the issues that are bothering you and try your best to be happy for both your spouse and yourself. They will feel more at ease and it will be simpler to be around you if you are joyful and pleasant to be around.

Maintaining your self-importance above your spouse, career, company, friends, and even your children is one of the most crucial pieces of marital preservation advice. It would be better if you took care of yourself as well. You would notice a change in your spouse and your marriage if you got a haircut, worked out, dressed to impress, and kept up with your personal cleanliness. It takes two to tango, so whenever you feel your spouse's anger or resentment toward you or toward you, speak out. Spend time discussing problems and determining the causes of any misunderstandings you two may have if you want to learn how to mend a marriage. Without criticising your spouse, acknowledge your contribution to the misunderstanding and apologise for your errors.

Thinking before you speak and using as few words as you can to get your idea through are the keys to effective communication. This keeps you focused and prevents you from coming across as argumentative or nagging, both of which can lead to an argument or cause your spouse to lose patience with you or speak over you. Additionally, it makes your idea simple to comprehend, resulting in fewer misunderstandings and uncertainty. Avoiding lengthy discussions will improve communication and make your "talks" less intimidating.

Find the source of your internal dissatisfaction, rage, and disappointment. You need to determine when you stopped caring about your relationship and why trying to repair it became so challenging. Determine what led you to give up on your relationship by listing all the problems. Try to communicate your concerns and desires for a solution to the issues with your partner. Put your attention on what can be mended rather than what is wrong in the relationship. Couples who begin to take one another for granted may make one another feel unappreciated and unimportant.

You must take action if you want to figure out how to salvage your marriage, so begin here! You are aware that you have the key. Your marriage's issues won't get better on their own. So, if you're still considering how I can save my marriage on my own, stop thinking about it and go to work. There are several marriage-saving suggestions available that might potentially help you reignite your marriage, so start somewhere. It's way too simple to let the affection in a marriage fade because of our busy lifestyles and even just growing accustomed to things over time. Couples must increase marital closeness in order to discover how to modify themselves in order to save their marriage.

Positive new beginnings are not heralded by power struggles, apathy, or attempts to alter the equations that further exacerbate disparities. Why would you want a new beginning with someone with whom a relationship is/was unpleasant or dull in the first place? is the most obvious question. People who are in love often act in the oddest, kindest, most honourable, and most unusual ways. It also promotes healing. It aids in overcoming trauma, anxieties, and destructive routines. Fights occur in every relationship. Every partnership experiences moments of suffering and hurt. For fresh starts to actually be new, you also need to learn how to let go. It doesn't help to keep repeating how damaged everything is. Discuss it, find a solution, then let it go. Happy fresh starts to everyone who wants them!

You must realise that pleading, sobbing, or just looking for approval won't help you alter anything while you're trying to figure out "how to preserve my marriage by myself." It would be advisable to stop using these coping mechanisms right now and start controlling your situation. It would be beneficial if you battled for it and took constructive action. The strategies you may take to manage your failing marriage should be discussed with your partner. You must act immediately and take all the required steps if you truly want to understand how to mend your marriage. You could start to question your abilities and wonder things like, "How can I save my marriage on my own?" or "Why am I doing this?" In any situation, though, you can not give up. You must have the fortitude to battle this by yourself. If you're eager to accept the task of "saving my marriage by myself," be aware that the path will be tough and lengthy.

Try to do little things to cheer up your companion. You may even play some indoor games together or make each other small treats like cake, drinks, and other foods.

Keep in mind that you must start making contributions to your marriage if you want it to be successful and for your partner to do the same. Everything that has to be done is done in a partnership. Therefore, if you want your marriage to improve, you must start the transformation.

Even though social media may have a positive influence on people, certain unfavourable consequences may cause issues in your romantic or marital relationships. Social media might lead to arguments between spouses because of fears of privacy invasion, time consumption, stalking, and addiction. Limit the amount of time you spend on social media and try to comprehend the harm it does. Let's face it: at some point or another, we have all engaged in social media stalking. Everyone is curious about a person's employment information, marital status, and travel plans. This urge to be aware of other people's affairs makes you feel incompetent and lowers your self-esteem.

Before contemplating ending a relationship, consider the reasons you fell in love with your spouse. Wedding vows are more than simply a few words; they serve as a reminder of your relationship's core principles and your own priorities. Marriage vows serve as a reminder of your reasons for choosing your spouse, your favourite aspects of them, and how they affect your shared life. They serve as a reminder to keep going even when things are challenging. Be realistic about your ability to achieve perfection.

Remember that no one is flawless while you're pondering "How to save my marriage by myself." Regardless of how kind and decent you are, you will still fall short of perfection. Everybody has some imperfections, and those weaknesses are what make us human. In order to find your spouse perfect, evaluate your own behaviour as well. Start embracing the imperfections in your relationship rather than expecting them to be flawless. You'll notice a shift in your conduct toward them as soon as you start doing it. You'll eventually get well, and your marriage will be in a better position.

One should be aware that nobody in this world, including you, me, and everyone else, is flawless. No marriage in our world is blissful. But do you understand what the trick is? You ought to take pleasure in all the minor pleasures life has to offer. You should accept your mate despite all of their defects and flaws. And by doing this, it would be extremely simple for you to obtain marital satisfaction. But what if your marriage isn't making you happy? So you made a mistake. One finds enjoyment in all of the connections he makes in life, whether they be with friends, relatives, cousins, or romantic partners. As a result, examine your life and inner self. Discover your self-worth, and then seek to increase it. Your married life will be filled with love, happiness, and calm as a result.

On a lighter note, marriages are forged in heaven. However, so are hail, tornadoes, lightning, and thunder.

About The Author

Dr. Amit is the founder of Accumentors India, a consultancy firm set up by him in the human resource solutions space, which is focused on developing processes for people. It offers consultancy in learning management, mentorship, performance coaching, training and development, psychometric analysis, HR processes and interventions.

Dr. Amit Das is an experienced training and learning professional with more than 25 years of working history in the healthcare, medical devices, and learning management industries. Dr. Amit is a seasoned training professional with rich experience and a successful track record in aligning learning and training solutions to key business strategy with a strong focus on flawless execution excellence to facilitate individual, business divisional, and organizational performance. He maintains a laser-like focus on training impact and ROI, people capability graphs, training process governance, performance coaching, and strategic thinking.These have been some of his key individual success traits. His core capabilities include performance coaching, designing training and development frameworks and facilitation of technical skill building, psychometric assessment and analysis, competency framework development and assessments, content design and facilitation of soft skills and leadership programs, E-Learning Platform development, Learning Management Systems, Learning Impact Measurement, Talent Analysis and Performance Management System Review, Performance Coaching and Counselling. Dr. Amit Das is a renowned executive advisor, consultant, author, speaker, and coach whose 25 years of business experience provides high-impact, practical solutions that support his clients' leadership development and organizational transformations. Dr. Amit Das is recognized as an innovative, principled thought leader who combines intellectual rigor and discipline with an ability to translate theory into practice. His operational skills are coupled with a strategic ability to analyze, develop, and implement successful strategies for profitability, growth, and sustainability.

For almost 25 years, the author has been at the forefront of introducing positive psychology techniques to organizations all throughout India. He presents compelling neuroscience studies in his programs that demonstrate that success does not precede pleasure; rather, the reverse is true. He has assisted thousands of individuals in increasing their levels of pleasure at work and has assisted managers and executives in leading with good emotions to boost team performance. He finds great satisfaction in fostering happier and more energizing settings for others to work in. His interests are in the areas of leadership development, coaching competency, mentorship, and motivational complexities related to organizational issues. His hobbies include public speaking, content creation, and reading books.

He has a Ph.D. and a Fellowship in strategic learning, along with his first class degrees in Human Resource Management, Marketing Management, International Business, and Corporate Law from the top business schools. He is a certified professional coach from the U.K. and a behavioral coach from the U.S.A. He is also certified Talent Analyst, HR Analyst, NLP Practitioner, Psychologist, Black Belt in LSS.

References

- *Marriage Advice self-help books: Communication in Marriage Workbook by Katerina Griffith, April 2022*
- *Together Forever God's Design for Marriage: Premarital Counseling Mentor's Guide by Ed Wright and Angie Wright, November 2017*
- *30 Secrets of Success in Marriage: A Book for Premarital and Marriage Counseling by Githiga, September 2019*
- *Supreme Court on Marriage & Divorce, Cruelty/Dowry Death, Custody, Adoption & Maintenance (1950 to 2016) (In 2 Volumes) by Surendra Malik and Sudeep Malik, 2016 Edition*
- *Marriage Counseling 101: The Five Step Action Plan to a Happy & Healthy Marriage. Increase the Joy of Sanctity, Safety, and Stability in Your Home by Rabbi Shlomo Slatkin, Jan 2020 ·*
- *The Husbands and Wives Club: A Year in the Life of a Couples Therapy Group written by Laurie Abraham and narrated By: Laural Merlington, March 2010*
- *Couples Therapy Workbook (Paperback), By Kathleen Mates-youngman, Mates-Youngman Kathleen Mates-Youngman, Pesi Publishing & Media, Oct 2014*
- *Introduction to Couple Therapy and Counseling by Hattem Abbi, 2015*
- *Couples in Conflict: A Family Systems Approach to Marriage Counselling Paperback by Ronald W. Richardson , October 2010*
- *Anxiety in Relationship + Insecure in Love + Toxic Relationship + Narcissistic Relationship + Couples Communication + Relationship Questions for Couples by A. P. Collins , narrated by: Melanie Strickland, Clare Radix, April 2017*
- *His Needs, Her Needs, Building a Marriage That Lasts written by: Dr. Willard F. Harley Jr. and narrated by: Dr. Willard F. Harley Jr., March 2019*
- *Couple Counselling outlines the essential principles and practices of couple counselling. Demystifying this form of therapy, the author*

provides a step-by-step guide by Martin Payne, June 2018

- *Marriage Counseling Workbook For Couples: 20 Ways To Rekindle The Love In Your Marriage by Dr Jane Smart, September 2019*
- *Together Forever God's Design for Marriage: Premarital Counseling Mentor's Guide by Ed Wright and Angie Wright, November 2017*
- *Hope-Focused Marriage Counseling: A Guide to Brief Therapy by Everett L. Worthington, August 2005*
- *Marriage Counseling: A Practical Guide for Pastors and Counselors by H. Norman Wright, May 1995*
- *Marriage Counseling: The Brilliant Philosophical Guide For Having An Everlasting Marriage (Professional advice on how to help your marriage last) by Rebecca R. Stone, September 2016*
- *The Role of Religion in Marriage and Family Counseling (Routledge Series on Family Therapy and Counseling) by Jill Duba Onedera, February 2015*
- *The First Years of Forever (Pyranee Books) by Ed Wheat and Gloria Okes Perkins, November 1988*
- *Coming Apart: How to Heal Your Broken Heart (Uncoupling, Divorce, Move On) by Daphne Rose Kingma, 24 November 2020*
- *The Marriage Counseling Workbook: 8 Steps to a Strong and Lasting Relationship by Emily Cook PhD LCMFT, 27 February 2018*
- *Marriage Counseling by Ashley Diaz, July 2017*
- *Effective Marriage Counseling: The His Needs, Her Needs Guide to Helping Couples by Willard F. Harley Jr., February 2010*
- *Gospel-Centered Marriage Counseling: An Equipping Guide for Pastors and Counselors by Robert W. PhD Kellemen and Jeremy Pierre, September 2020*
- *Marriage Counseling and Anxiety in relationship: Practical Guide for Making Marriage Work, How to Eliminate Insecurity and Jealousy, Reduce Conflicts, and Reconnect with Your Partner by Ester Novak, May 2020*
- *Marriage Counseling : Family Life (1 Book 40) by Emmanuel Matthew Agada August 2020*
- *Marriage Counseling 101: A Practical Guide For Ministers by Patsy Highland March 2009*

- *Marriage Counseling Secrets: 7 Heart Winning Secrets of Improving Communication with Your Spouse and Build a Long-lasting Relationship by Goldink Books, October 2021*
- *Marriage Counseling Secrets: 7 Heart Winning Secrets of Improving Communication with Your Spouse and Build a Long-lasting Relationship by Goldink Books, October 2021*
- *Saving Your Marriage Before It Starts Workbook for Men: Seven Questions to Ask Before---And After---You Marry by Les and Leslie Parrott, November 2015*
- *Marriage Counseling: Practical Guide for Making Marriage Work Building a Strong and Lasting Relationship by Ester Novak, August 2019*
- *Marriage Counseling: Tips about Sexual Intimacy, Communication, Sex Differences, Family, and More by Charissa Felts, February 2020*
- *Marriage: The Secret To Rebuilding Trust, Intimacy, and Connection in your marriage (Marriage Help, Marriage Advice, Marriage Counseling, Wife, Husband, Relationships) by Karen Johnson, April 2016*
- *Marriage: How to be Better at Marriage and Rebuild Connection, Intimacy, and Love. (Marriage help, Marriage counseling, Love, Intimacy, Marriage tips) by Karen Soloman, February 2016*
- *Marriage Counseling: How to Communicate with, Forgive, and Love Your Partner by Charissa Felts, February 2020*
- *Marriage Counseling: Ways To Save Your Marriage: Solve Marital Problems & Enjoy A Longer, Happier Marriage by Viola Richardson and Sean Conway, |June 2015*
- *Making Your Marriage Work: Maama's Practical Wisdom For A Lasting, Happy Marriage by Eyitayo Dada, September 2017*
- *Marriage Counseling: The Real Truth About Marriage by Gloria Hunsaker, September 2015*
- *Marriage: How to Keep Your Marriage and Love Going for Life (Marriage, Marriage Counseling Guide, Marriage Help Book 1) by Heather William, November 2016*
- *Marriage: How To Start A New Beginning, Embrace Your Differences And Deepen Your Bond (Marriage, Marriage Counseling, Marriage*

Help, Romance, Love, Happiness, Marriage Books) by Wizardson Inc, July 2016

- *I Have a Plan: A Pastor's Guide to Counseling Troubled Marriages by Charles L. Rassieur, August 2005*
- *Maturity in marriages & Relationships : Marriage counseling workbooks for couples & new rules of marriage and family & marriage devotional for couples by Williams . A Robert, June 2022*
- *Marriage Advice self-help books: Communication in Marriage Workbook And Marriage Counseling Workbook by Katerina Griffith, April 2022*
- *Marriage with Meaning: A Values-Based Model for Premarital Counseling by Rabbi Daniel Young, December 2010*
- *Marriage Counseling Workbook For Couples: 20 Ways To Rekindle The Love In Your Marriage: 1 (Marriage and Relationship Therapy) by Dr Jane Smart, September 2019*
- *Healing Your Spouse After Your Affair: How To Truly Understand Things From Your Partner's Perspective And Provide The Needed Support by Laura Redmond, March 2021*
- *Marriage Counseling for Couples: On How to Fix Your Marriage: Simple Principles of a Happy Marriage, the Blueprint by Lucy Vialli, August 2014*
- *Marriage: How To Save Your Marriage And Rebuild Connection, Intimacy and Trust By Understanding It Better (Marriage Help, Marriage Counseling, Intimacy Advice, Relationship Communication Book 1) by Cory Spring, |March 2016*
- *Sex and Marriage: More Sex, Passion and Desire for Married Couples: Discover the 10 Ways to Turn Your Sex Life From Routine to Lustful Desire (Sex Tips, Marriage Counseling) by Rochelle Foxx, March 2015*
- *Marriage Counseling: The Go to Guide for Marriage Problems by Jeremy Lozano, September 2015*
- *Marriage Counseling: Helpful Ways To Build Security In Marriage! by Shawn Jackson, June 2022*
- *Marriage Counseling: How To Fall In Love Again - Marriage Rescue, Stay In Love, Intimacy In Marriage & Marriage Recovery (Stay In Love, Marriage Rescue, ... Intimacy In Marriage, Marriage Problems)*

by Samantha Morgan, | January 2014

- *The Anxious Lover: Overcome Anxiety, Manage Conflicts and Improve Your Relationship by Nora Williams, November 2021*
- *30 Secrets of Success in Marriage: A Book for Premarital and Marriage Counseling by Githiga, September 2019*
- *Marriage Counseling: Surviving a Broken Heart, Divorce, or Love Depression by Charissa Felts, February 2020*
- *Marriage: How to Rescue, Revive and Rebuild Trust in Your Marriage (Marriage Counseling, Intimacy Advice, Marriage Help Book 1)by Robert Young, December 2016*
- *Marriage Counseling: Interesting Facts I Bet You Never Knew by Angela Click, January 2016*
- *Marriage Counseling: The Complete Guide For Couples by Eugene Erker, May 2022*
- *Laugh Your Way to a Better Marriage: Unlocking the Secrets to Life, Love, and Marriage by Mark Gungor, March 2009*
- *Marriage Success Handbook: 22 Critical Lessons Church Folks Should Learn About Dating, Sex, and Marriage by Dr David F Stephens, March 2007*
- *Healing Your Spouse After Your Affair: How To Truly Understand Things From Your Partner's Perspective And Provide The Needed Support by Laura Redmond, March 2021*
- *Marriage Counseling: Simple Relationship Advice to Help Bring Intimacy Back into Your Love Life by K. Connors, June 2017*
- *Marriage on the Rock 25th Anniversary: The Comprehensive Guide to a Solid, Healthy and Lasting Marriage (Marriage on the Rock Book) by Jimmy Evans, September 2019*
- *Marriage Counseling: 2 Manuscripts - Relationship Growth, Codependency. How to Help a Flawed Relationship by Setting Healthy Boundaries, Improving Communication, Sex Life and More! by Jacob Costas, February 2019*
- *Marriage Counseling: 7 Steps To Discover Happiness In Marriage by Magdalen Braelynn Kelsey, April 2020*
- *Marriage: Your guide on how to make your marriage last and love your men unconditionally: (marriage counseling, relationships,*

communication) by Jacqueline De Maria and Jeanine Wormwood, February 2019

- *The Marriage Counseling Workbook: Guide to Effective Marriage Therapy and Communication Techniques for a Healthy and Long-Lasting Relationship by Katerina Griffith, April 2022*
- *Marriage Workbook for Couples: A Hope Focused Easy Marriage Counseling Games and Guidelines by Chris Brown, December 2021*
- *Marriage and Family Counseling: A Manual for Ministers, Doctors, Lawyers, Teachers, Social Workers, and Others Engaged in Counseling Service (Classic Reprint) by Sidney Emanuel Goldstein, November 2018*
- *Marriage Clarity: The Ultimate Marriage Counseling Workbook for Couples by Diane Clerk, October 2021*
- *20 Ways To Rekindle The Love In Your Marriage: A simple marriage counseling guide for couples (Love And Healthy Relationships) by Dr Jane Smart, February 2021*
- *Marriage Counseling Workbook: A Guide for Couples to Overcome Infidelity, Finding Love after Heartbreak and Communication Skills by Ridan Z. Mary, July 2020*
- *Marriage: Marriage Fix 1.0: The Ultimate Solution to Fix Your Marriage Problems in 7 Simple Steps...Now! (marriage help, marriage counseling, conflict resolution Book 1)by Alex Riches, June 2015*
- *Saving Your Marriage Before It Starts Workbook for Women Updated: Seven Questions to Ask Before---and After---You Marry by Les and Leslie Parrott, November 2015*
- *Marriage Counseling: 5 Ways To Make Your Boring Marriage Wild Again! by Brin English, January 2015*
- *Marriage: Learn Relationship And Marriage Secrets To Creating A Deeper, More Fulfilling, Lasting Marriage, Forever (Counseling, secrets, love, help, divorce, communication, marriage) by Ben Pierce, December 2015*
- *Marriage: How to be a good wife: 7 things you Must Know to fix your marriage and have a happy relationship (restore intimacy, joy, marriage counseling, marriage advice, marriage help) by Grace May,*

November 2015

- *Marriage Counseling That Works: Simple Marriage Help Techniques To Bring Love, Trust And Intimacy Back Into Your Life (Marriage Advice, Relationship Issues, Relationship Rescue) by Victor Anderson, April 2014*
- *How To Save Marriage From Divorce: Complete Guide on Marriage Counseling for Couples Husband Wife Men Women by ARX Reads, April 2022*
- *Marriage: The Honeymoon Is Over, Now What? (Does your Marriage need help, need counseling? Get this guide first.) (Marriage Today Book 1) by Mary Peters, June 2014*
- *Saving Your Marriage: Fall In Love Again (fighting for your marriage, marriage advice, couples, prevent divorce, marriage counseling) by Jamie Monroe, September 2015*

Printed by Libri Plureos GmbH in Hamburg,
Germany